TRUE TALES
PARANORMAL

T0221613

TRUE TALES OF THE
PARANORMAL
SPIRITS, GHOSTS AND THE HIDDEN WORLD

NEIL WARD

This edition published in 2024 by Arcturus Publishing Limited
26/27 Bickels Yard, 151–153 Bermondsey Street,
London SE1 3HA

Copyright © Arcturus Holdings Limited

All rights reserved. No part of this publication may be reproduced, stored in a
retrieval system, or transmitted, in any form or by any means, electronic, mechanical,
photocopying, recording or otherwise, without prior written permission in accordance
with the provisions of the Copyright Act 1956 (as amended). Any person or persons
who do any unauthorised act in relation to this publication may be liable to criminal
prosecution and civil claims for damages.

AD011231UK

Printed in the UK

CONTENTS

INTRODUCTION
What is the paranormal? 7

CHAPTER ONE
Enchanters, strange visitors and prophetic dreams............. 17

CHAPTER TWO
Hospitalized spirits, psychic doctors and life-savers........... 51

CHAPTER THREE
Hauntings, strange messages and time slips 73

CHAPTER FOUR
Fake seances and true mediumship 101

CHAPTER FIVE
Amazing readings and help from ETs?............................. 129

CHAPTER SIX
Hearing voices, spirit communication and the Church..... 159

CHAPTER SEVEN
Science investigates the paranormal 193

CHAPTER EIGHT
Door handles to a new frontier.. 219

CONCLUSION
The ghosts of tomorrow 241

INDEX... 249

PICTURE CREDITS 255

INTRODUCTION

WHAT IS THE PARANORMAL?

The 'paranormal' describes events and experiences that cannot be explained by normal laws of science or reason. It includes ghosts, spirits, faeries, psychic phenomena, aliens, UFOs (unidentified flying objects), and other unexplained events. Throughout history, people have been fascinated with the subject, and it has played a significant role in shaping and expressing many different human cultures and beliefs. For example, the ancient Egyptians believed in the existence of earth-bound ghosts and in spirits of the dead, while the ancient Greeks believed their gods and goddesses could appear and disappear at will. Today, millions of people around the world firmly maintain that they can communicate with the spirits of deceased loved ones via a clairvoyant medium, have been plagued by troublesome poltergeists, or have seen or even been abducted temporarily by alien beings. (In 2022 NASA itself tasked a dedicated team to examine data on UFOs, or what it calls UAPs – 'unidentified aerial phenomena', which we'll see more of later in the book.)

WATCHERS AND WATCHED

Every day, it seems that someone, somewhere experiences an unusual encroachment into their 'normal' world, or glimpses another existence beyond the one we all inhabit on this planet. This book delves into the accounts of those who have actually come face to face with this 'other'. While their rarity is partly what makes these stories so fascinating, many of us have experienced the feeling, that odd shiver of instinct, that someone, or something, is there and is watching – but frustratingly, we can't see them, or it. Materialists and scientists will no doubt attribute this to human brain chemistry going into overdrive and putting the body on alert just in case there is a threat hiding nearby.

In my view such experiences are a personal kind of evidence of the planes of existence beyond our own. The stories in this book suggest that the supernatural exists beyond our world but also within and alongside it. In some instances, they suggest the spirit world, or afterlife, is watching and sometimes even asserting itself in what may seem like strange or unnerving ways, but which are often for our benefit. For me, these stories serve as clear evidence that our reality intersects with myriad others that are 'paranormal' to us. Theoretical physics has indicated that there are dimensions that exist or run parallel to our own. They do not state what could be in those other existences – however, various accounts of the supernatural give us some clues that perhaps beings such as faeries, ghosts and spirits come from those realms. They seem to have their own laws of physics and things like time do not have the same meaning for those living there. In Chapter 8 we will even consider a theory that seeks to explain that all these dimensions are likely, in fact, to be part of one unified super energy.

Encounters with the supernatural generate reactions in people ranging from awe and wonder to fear and anxiety. Ghost sightings, for example, can leave some people feeling uneasy or even traumatized, while UFO sightings can leave some feeling so excited and curious they start searching for more answers. This book recounts the experiences of people from all walks of life and from around the world who believe they have encountered the unexplained. We will see how these experiences have been interpreted in the past and how they are viewed in light of modern technology's ability to 'see' and describe strange phenomena – and make contact with it. We will also examine similarities and potential links between different kinds of paranormal event: how, for example, UFOs and spirits might actually connect, and how one might provide a partial explanation for the other. Additionally, we will explore interpretations of what the paranormal might be, and suggest that our current approach to physics might be in need of a rethink, or at least an update.

Despite the paranormal defying scientific minds and explanations in the usual sense, in the last 150 years or so a small pocket of science has begun to unwrap the mystery of the supernatural. We will examine this in more detail later on in the book, considering some of those scientists who have researched paranormal claims more seriously, changing their own world view in the process.

WHO IS THIS BOOK FOR?

There is much we do not yet understand about the world around us. Some of the most brilliant and highly rational individuals in history, including Sir Arthur Conan Doyle and Winston Churchill, expressed a belief in particular aspects of the paranormal. There is an array of evidence out there that could convince even the most hardened sceptic, if only they were willing to engage with it. This book is intended, then, for the open-minded enquirer who is willing to consider both the testimony of people who claim to have actually experienced the paranormal and different ways of interpreting the more unusual elements of our world.

In several instances there seem to be patterns of experience in these accounts, which makes them all the more intriguing and, it can be argued, less likely to have been fabricated. For example, some encounters seem to be almost designed for only one witness – who is prevented from alerting others by some strange force, or whose companions simply can't see the paranormal event or being. British researcher and writer Jenny Randles coined the phrase 'the Oz factor' to describe the feeling that UFO witnesses have reported during their encounters, of being inside their own time and reality bubble, totally transfixed. In some cases the witness finds that in reality a few hours have passed, although they weren't aware of this because somehow their memories have been tampered with. Some encounters with faerie-type beings share similar features (see Chapter 1) and researcher Jacques Valle was one of the first to make a comparison between the two, and to speculate whether they could be one and the same experience.

Some of the accounts in this book come from those people who feel they are 'sensitive' to the paranormal – that is, they may have psychic abilities that allow them to apprehend more than most. But many are the recollections of 'ordinary' people, some of whom would no doubt have said they didn't believe in anything paranormal – and maybe still don't!

The 'sensitive' or 'psychic' terms indicate that these witnesses in most cases have a sixth sense, one that they themselves are usually not fully aware of. Just as ordinary people have different abilities, such as musical, artistic or mathematical skills, the 'psychics' and 'sensitives' also have their own range of psychic abilities. They have a knack of knowing what is about to happen, or the ability to perceive a spirit, or feel the presence of otherworldly beings. The individual mind of each person will have their own unique blueprints of what they can do or perceive, but those blueprints, with time and practice, can be expanded and new skills can be learned. The term 'psychic' does not refer only to the ability to tell the future, but covers many areas of intuition and the ability to know or see or feel things beyond what

Jenny Randles, renowed Ufologist who coined the idea of the 'Oz factor'.

is generally accepted. The stories and accounts in this book show a broad range of those abilities.

The stories that follow will interest all of those with a yearning and curiosity to learn more about what is really going on out there, whether because they suspect they might possess these abilities themselves or they simply want to learn more about the mysteries of the world around them.

A PERSONAL INTEREST

I include myself among the open-minded enquirers who I hope will greatly enjoy this book. As well as writing about the paranormal, I have also organized numerous demonstrations of spirit mediumship. My interest in the paranormal is personal as well as professional, arising from an encounter with the unknown which to this day I still can't explain as anything other than a true tale of the paranormal.

It begins with my mother Margaret. It was 2016 and I happened to be staying at my parents' house at the time she died. Although it was a normal day, I'd had an uneasy feeling that something was going to happen. That night, Mum passed away as the result of an aortic aneurysm. Thankfully, it was almost instant and she did not suffer much.

A month earlier, my brother had a strange experience: he woke up one night and saw a vision of our Mum coming through the door of his bedroom. She looked about 40 years younger and, smiling, she skipped silently through his room and past him, like a silent movie, then vanished out of the bedroom window. Mum was at that point still very much alive. My brother and I later speculated that this could have been a part of her consciousness stretching its wings, so to speak, and making a practice run out of the body in preparation for her passing.

From at least the Victorian era, there have been reports of sightings of ghosts or spirits of people who have not died. Many of these were reported in a book by Edmund Gurney, Frederic W.H. Myers and Frank Podmore called *Phantasms of the Living*.

About ten months later I found myself at a seance, sitting with a group of other people and two mediums in front of a Ouija board (a wooden board typically with the letters of the alphabet, numbers one to ten, and 'yes' and 'no' printed on it). Everyone placed one finger on an upturned wine glass on the board and the glass began to move. As it noisily scraped across the surface, it indicated that there was someone whose name began with the letter 'M' who wanted to talk to me.

'Hi son,' the glass spelled out. I was obviously excited to hear from my mum and as the session progressed it seemed as though she was just as excited as me! She gave her name as 'Margaret' and then correctly spelled out 'Bryan', my father's name, with a 'Y'. Then came the words 'I miss you.' (I was fascinated to know that the dead appear to miss the living.) I then asked her if she had met her own parents in the spirit world. 'Yes,' she replied, the glass whizzing around to spell, 'My mum came and met me.' She confirmed my brother's name as 'Philip' and the name of the road where she had lived as 'Lovel Road'. All of this was totally correct. She closed the session by saying that the other side was a place of 'loveliness'.

'LIVE LIFE TO THE FULL'

It wasn't just me that received a message – others at the seance also made contact with loved ones using the same board. Hayley's father had passed suddenly in 2018, which devastated her close family. Although still grieving her beloved dad's loss, Hayley was surprised and happy to hear from him – and took the opportunity to ask him if he would dictate a speech for his son Billy's wedding day.

On the day in question, Hayley read out the following message at Billy's wedding reception: 'Billy, you're not only the best son anyone could ask for, you are and will always be my best mate. For that, I will be forever grateful. Son, I am here by your side, watching you both have the greatest day of your lives. Don't ever say I am not here. I am, and I am the proudest man who is not on this Earth. To all that have been invited today, enjoy your special day! I love you all! Dad, your best mate. Live life to the full.'

Now, sceptics will say that mediums and psychics have no supernatural abilities and are just highly skilled at 'cold reading' people: that is, rapidly analyzing their words and body language to get enough information to make vague but broadly correct statements about their loved ones. This may work together with the 'Forer effect', where people desperate for a connection with a deceased loved one will deliberately interpret such statements in a way that backs up their belief in the spirit realm. Could this need also be the reason why someone could unconsciously move the wine glass on a Ouija board? This book will include lots of stories about paranormal accounts that are both compelling and likely to provoke debate on issues such as this!

Whether those messages that Hayley and I received were genuine or not is impossible to know. What is clear, though, is that they offered real comfort to us both. And their accuracy is difficult to explain scientifically or in terms that could be described as natural or normal. In this sense,

Ouija boards are marked with letters and numbers which allow spirits to communicate with the living.

they, and the many other incidents explored in this book, are beyond –
or 'para' – normal.

CHAPTER ONE

ENCHANTERS, STRANGE VISITORS AND PROPHETIC DREAMS

Every individual's encounter with the paranormal is a deeply personal experience, but it's fascinating to note, once you delve into their narratives, how many of these accounts seems to draw from a common fund of what we can think of as 'folk memory'. This is a kind of collective consciousness that connects us to a past, a time before history, when, some believe, our earliest ancestors lived in harmony with nature and with the faeries, sprites, little people, divine beings, mythical beasts and visitors from other worlds who existed in it alongside us.

In this version of the past, the folk tales, traditions and mythology that have been passed down to us are more than metaphors. They are chronicles of actual events and the biographies of real beings who once moved among us – and who, according the people whose stories are told in this chapter, still do. Our first accounts cover encounters with faerie-type beings: shy but curious creatures, often in partially human form and widely thought to watch humans. But what actually are they? This is a difficult question, as descriptions of them vary greatly and stories of these beings have come to us from around the world, so despite the accounts, we have no 'official' understanding of what they are.

Faerie legends run far back into the history of Europe, in whose varying cultures they were called, among other names, wee folk, fey, faeries, elementals, small people and spirits of nature. They may be identified with natural elements like water and trees, or the spirit world. For example, in Irish folklore *sidhe* are supernatural beings who live alongside humans but are invisible. They use their powerful magic to help or punish humans who are able to see them, depending on whether the humans please or offend them.

The word 'faerie' comes from a centuries-old English word meaning a magical enchantment or enchanted land, itself related to the old French 'fae', or supernatural being. With this in mind, it's interesting that in some of the following accounts 'enchantment' is actually the condition that people found themselves in: while perceiving

In Fairlyand, *1897 by Charles Rennie Mackintosh.*

such a being they seem to feel totally absorbed and focused in that moment. It's as if they are hypnotized – not by the swing of a watch, but by the swing of reality into another realm – which certainly sounds like a form of enchantment. Such 'glamour', as it is also sometimes called, often affects the witness, but sometimes seems to place others with them into some kind of strange trance.

A STRANGE FASCINATION

In mid-1970s Iran a soldier, Hussain Parsa, was patrolling the streets at night with a fellow soldier when a sandstorm blew up. Finding shelter in a mosque, they both removed their shoes and Hussain's friend slept while he kept a lookout. Hussain had inadvertently drifted off to sleep but suddenly woke up and was shocked to see a mysterious woman and girl were now sitting in front of them and staring intently at Hussain's feet and those of his colleague. Hussain tried to discreetly elbow his sleeping colleague awake but no matter how hard he shoved with his elbow, his friend did not even stir. Then the woman looked up from his feet and stared straight at Hussain. He said, 'I knew as soon as I looked into her eyes that she was not of this world.' Without warning, the strange woman and girl stood up and walked away. 'As they walked away,' he said, 'I noticed they both had cloven-hoofed feet and then they vanished into the wall of the mosque.'

Hussain's mysterious visitors seemed to be fascinated with human feet, as if they were the oddity in this reality. Legends of the past suggest humans met similar beings such as Pan, a supposed devil-like beings with hooves and a tail. Pan was the Greek god of shepherds and hunters, and of the meadows and forests of the mountain wilds. His unseen presence aroused panic in those who traversed his realm. This is where the word 'panic' originates from. Could these strange visitors who entranced Hussain be a kind of faerie being?

*Pan, the mythological Greek creature with horns and cloven hooves,
may appear unexpectedly from time to time.*

One encounter with Pan was reported by scientist R. Ogilvie Crombie (known as Roc), who claimed to have met a faun being called Kurmos. The first time the Scotsman encountered the 1 m (3 ft) tall creature was at the Royal Botanic Gardens in Edinburgh in 1966. Roc said: 'I saw with astonishment that it was a faun, the Greek mythological being, half human, half animal. He had a pointed chin and ears and two little horns on his forehead. His shaggy legs ended in cloven hooves…' That initial encounter was, however, just a stepping stone to another encounter about a month later, on the island of Iona in Scotland. There, Roc saw Pan through the grass. At first, he appeared to look like a monk in a brown habit with the hood pulled over his head.

The tall being raised his hands and rolled back the hood to reveal himself as Pan. He rose up out of the ground and stood facing Roc, who described him as an immense figure at least 7.5 m (25 ft) tall. The Pan being said to Roc he was 'the servant of Almighty God, and he and his subjects would come to the aid of mankind, in spite of the way it has treated them and abused nature'.

Some traditions identify faerie-like beings more with the undead and malign activities such as drinking human blood, stealing away human children or even shadows, seen as representing a person's soul. And if you believe the next account, this still happens today.

SHADOW THIEVES

In the summer of 1997, Steve Odale from Glasgow was on a visit to Schiehallion Mountain (known locally as 'Fairy Hill') near the Cairngorms National Park in Scotland. It was nearly 5pm; the sun was low in the sky and the soft, light, gauzy clouds and shimmering rain created a lovely rainbow over the hills. Steve stood there watching the rainbow emerging over the mountain. Nearby, he said, a stream running down the hillside started to sound more like music than trickling water.

As he looked up at the rainbow and listened to the 'music', Steve began to feel rather enchanted by the ethereal tune. This feeling was probably the key to his experience.

He was distracted by a movement in his peripheral vision. He glanced down at his feet and was astonished to see a small woman about 1 m (3 ft) in height, with brown leathery skin and a small leather pointed hat. She was holding what appeared to be an old pair of sheep shears and was proceeding to cut around the sole of Steve's shoes. Looking at the cast of his shadow up the mountain, Steve saw a similar being that appeared to be the male equivalent of the small woman. The male being was holding the end of Steve's shadow and rolling it up as if it were a sheet of paper! Steve was so astonished at the sight that he was only able to shout 'Oi!' The beings looked at each other, apparently surprised they could be seen, and vanished instantly.

Steve described the beings as resembling the incredibly well-preserved bodies buried thousands of years ago in Norwegian peat bogs, their skin having a brown, leathery look. The female had partial facial hair and very dirty nails, and wore poorly sewn, ragged leather-like clothes and a small pointy hat. The obvious questions are what were they and why would they want his shadow?

Steve's description of the female being is especially interesting, such as having dirty nails: as well as being able to vanish, suggesting an existence outside our reality, the dirt in her nails and her clothing point to these beings also existing on a physical level in our world. They may kill and skin animals to fabricate their clothes, for example.

As to why the two beings wanted his shadow, some traditions identify a person's shadow with their soul – should they lose it, they lose control over their thoughts and actions, becoming like the undead themselves. It certainly seems like the shadow was of some importance to them. Alternatively, maybe these little people were helping Steve by removing negative energies. Whatever the truth of this account, our earthly reality appears to be important to the beings Steve described. By shouting at them, he appeared to break the effect of the enchantment – thereby breaking its power over him.

A MUSICAL PICNIC

In 1975, Mary Rose Julian and her young daughter April were at their family's favourite picnic spot in a remote wooded area by a lake in Nova Scotia, Canada. While paddling with April and her other children, Mary Rose became aware of a strange noise, which she described as like a kind of music. She instinctively felt they needed to get away from the

Schiehallion Mountain, or Fairy Hill, in Cairngorms National Park, Scotland.

area and asked her daughter if she could hear the musical sound too. April replied that she could.

Now certain that she was not hearing things, Mary Rose quickly got April and her other children out of the water and back into the car. As the panicked mother started the engine, she urged her daughter, 'Don't look back, look at me.' April, however, was more curious and decided to look out of the window. She saw a small being coming out of the woods to join a group of similar beings who were already formed into a circle. She later described them as looking semi-transparent and almost camouflaged, like they were partly merging into the environment. They appeared to be dancing and skipping around and they were singing some kind of tune. It was this sound that Mary Rose and April first heard when they were paddling in the lake.

Of course, April could have read about faeries or similar creatures in stories and brought them from imagination into life. Mary Rose didn't see the strange beings herself, and most of us would sense danger more readily if something odd were to happen in an isolated location.

However, in Mary Rose's case, it was the strange musical tones and singing that she heard which caused her to become very cautious.

Different countries across Europe have their own variations of folklore around magical creatures dancing. In English and Celtic traditions, a circle of mushrooms in woodland is often called a 'faerie ring' as these were believed to have been caused by faeries or elves dancing in a circle. Some traditions say that if humans step inside the circle, or see the dance, they will be forced to dance until exhaustion or death, or even stolen away, whereas others see the rings as a sign of good fortune.

What would have happened if Mary Rose and April had continued paddling in the lake? Would the enchanting music have enraptured them so that they too might have suffered an attempted shadow theft like Steve Odale's? If this was an enchantment spell, it appears to induce a kind of hypnotic light trance focusing on a key element (like music or a rainbow) to the exclusion of everything else – similar to a daydream, where the subconscious mind bypasses the ego and allows the mind to wander freely. Music often relaxes people into this state and perhaps the faerie music is used with similar intentions.

A typical 'faerie ring' of mushrooms growing in a circle.

THE WOLLATON GNOMES

Wollaton Park in Nottinghamshire was placed firmly on the map in September 1979 as one of the most famous locations for faerie-type encounters – this time with small beings known as 'The Wollaton Gnomes'. One of the witnesses, after encountering this strange sight, described the creatures as 'kinda like gnomes', and the name stuck. Local newspapers reported that six primary-school children claimed they saw up to 60 gnome-like creatures in the park, which forms part of the huge grounds around the Elizabethan Wollaton Hall estate. It was just starting to get dark and the children were playing at the edge of the park. Noticing some movement near the trees, they went to investigate and saw small lights, which then formed into gnome-like creatures who came out from behind the trees in what appeared to be small vehicles! The children estimated there were around 30 of these strange cars with two gnomes inside each.

The beings appeared to be about half the children's size and were old, with very wrinkled faces. They wore long, droopy blue hats and had long black beards with a red tip at the end. The 'cars', which had no wheels, were red and white, with a handle instead of a steering wheel and triangular-shaped headlamps or lights. The children said these vehicles were able to move quickly and chased them around the woods in a type of game. The 'gnomes' were laughing as they chased the children and did not appear to be intent on harming them. One child reported hearing them speak in a strange language. For some reason, these creatures only seemed to be able to chase the children so far. As they approached a gate at the edge of the park, where street lamps were by now illuminated, the gnomes would not follow them. The children felt that somehow, the bright electric lights posed a kind of danger to the small creatures.

It's interesting that a fear of sunlight is a characteristic associated with gnomes in different northern European countries' folklore. (Such beings include *nisse* or *tomte* in Scandinavia and *erdmannchen* in Germany.) Typically they are small and have a strong connection to the earth, often living underground or deep in forests and only emerging at night.

It would be easy to argue that the children were simply making it up. The hats, beards and Noddy-like cars could have come directly from children's books and animations. However, the children were later interviewed separately by their school's headmaster, who recorded each interview. All the witness accounts matched, except for one child stating the colour of the gnomes' beards as white, not black. So there appears to be something to this bizarre story, particularly in light of earlier events at Wollaton Park.

PREVIOUS GNOME ENCOUNTERS

Marjorie Johnson's *Seeing Faeries* reported that in 1900 a Mrs George was passing the same gate at the edge of Wollaton Park when she saw small men standing in the doorway to the lodge located there. To her, their clothing resembled that of policemen of the day, although they were only around 0.6–1 m (2–3 ft) tall. They also appeared to be friendly, smiling at her and looking very happy. In the mid-1950s a woman named Jean Dixon also became aware of gnome-like beings while walking in the same park. She claimed that they led her on a walk around the park, showing her things of interest.

Mark Fox, an author specializing in religion, spirituality and the paranormal, wrote that in 1930 his aunt Alma was living in a large house by the embankment of Wollaton Park. One fine day, Alma and a friend were enjoying a picnic by the lake when they saw some people no larger than dolls coming out from behind some bushes, dressed in fancy clothes. They travelled across the lake in a small boat, then they vanished behind bushes on the other side of the water. Sixty years later, a friend of Mark's told him that while visiting the same area with his girlfriend, they had spotted some tiny people by the edge of the lake, wearing waistcoats, pretty dresses and all in hats. When they were spotted, the beings vanished behind some bushes.

Wollaton Park, the site of one of the more notable instances of an encounter with gnomes.

While some of the visitors in these stories were more timid than others, one of the notable similarities is their friendly nature. Much of the European mythology around gnomes has described them as good-humoured and benevolent, if sometimes a little mischievous. The next group of paranormal tales concern strange visitors whose purpose may be to help humans in difficult, even tragic, situations.

SEEING CENTAURS

It was the early 2000s in a hospital in Lancashire, England. Joanne had given birth to a stillborn baby. She was placed in a hospital recovery room, with her baby beside her in a cot, so they could spend some precious time together before Joanne would have to let her baby go. She was, naturally, devastated and as she grieved she also worried about how she was ever going to be strong enough to cope with this tragedy, let alone help her family to do so while she felt so wounded and broken.

After a while, Joanne said she noticed a movement and four or five small centaur beings walked through the door into the room.

These strange creatures were about a foot and a half (45 cm) in height with the lower body of a horse, a human upper torso, and incredibly ugly faces! Two of the creatures walked over to the cot where the baby lay and looked inside at the tiny lifeless body. The others walked up to Joanne's bed and just stood there quietly, looking up at her, as she looked down at them in utter disbelief. She clearly remembered feeling that they weren't at all threatening or ill intentioned, but simply curious and somehow gracing her with their quiet, calm presence: so much so, that she did not speak or cry out but sat transfixed in the moment. After some time the beings vanished, although Joanne had no recollection of them walking out the door – they were just no longer in the room. After this visit, Joanne said something shifted in her frame of mind. She felt more positive and suddenly more willing and able to carry on with life for herself and her family.

The presence of the small centaurs seemed to have had a healing effect on Joanne. Interestingly, centaurs are often associated with healing powers. For example, in ancient Greek mythology the centaur Chiron was famed for his great knowledge of medicinal herbs, but when he was injured he chose to save Prometheus, the tortured Titan, instead of himself. Some writers speculate this story shows us that we can help ourselves through pain by helping others. Centaurs may also represent different aspects of our world and the conflict within us between reason and animal instinct. So perhaps these centaurs were not so out of place in a hospital after all.

Of course, an alternative viewpoint is that her highly emotional state, physical exhaustion after giving birth and pain medication caused Joanne to hallucinate the hybrid beings. But while pain relief wears off, this experience continued to help her. Maybe Joanne was able to see the centaurs because, unknown to her, she has some psychic abilities. Howard Hughes, who podcasts on mysterious events and the paranormal, recalled that as a youngster he was walking past the railway station in Liverpool with his grandmother, who was apparently gifted with 'second sight', or the ability to see future events. 'Don't look!' she suddenly told Howard. Being an inquisitive child, he decided he was going to look, and saw to his great surprise a cloven-hoofed man with a normal human head and torso, but a horse's lower body, walking along the pavement nearby. His grandmother presumably didn't want to alarm or frighten Howard by the sight of this cloven-hoofed man. Although Howard saw it along with his grandmother, no one else seemed to notice this strange creature. His grandmother's psychic ability – and young Howard's too – was the likely reason that they could see this creature. Their psychic ability was, it seemed, attuned to seeing things that others could not, namely, clairvoyance, the seeing of things

The centaur Chiron from a 1st century CE *Roman mosaic in Naples.*

beyond the physical realm. This being was possibly partly within the realm of the Earth, but just outside the perception of most people. In contrast to Howard's grandmother, some people are probably psychic but don't become aware of their unusual ability until something strange comes knocking, as our next story illustrates.

GUIDING SPIRIT

By 1992, Jan's husband had spent the last year of his life in Buckinghamshire needing an oxygen mask to breathe. One day, said Jan, as she was lifting him forward in bed to make him comfortable, he told her that he was in so much pain he just wanted to die. A moment later he passed away in her arms. Jan laid him back down on to their bed and noticed a kind of mist rise out of his chest and float upwards towards the ceiling. It then moved across the ceiling and vanished into the airing cupboard in the corner of the room.

Six months later, Jan woke up in the early hours in the same bedroom. 'I looked across at the cupboard,' she recalled, 'because I saw a Native American trying to climb out of it!' She could clearly see this spirit form, although only from the chest upwards. It was a male with war paint on his face, wearing a bone necklace and a headdress of feathers. He was moving his arms as if wading through water, trying to get out of the cupboard but not quite making it into the room. Jan also noticed the silhouette of a man behind the first spirit, and possibly a third man behind him who was wearing a hat. She could not make out any more details about them. This was not a one-off sighting. The same thing started to happen every night, waking Jan between 3am and 4am each time.

What was going on here? The term 'spirit guide' was not familiar to Jan as she had never visited a spiritualist church, where members of the public watch a medium demonstrate their ability to communicate with those that have passed through what we call death. Mediums often 'tune into' one or more spirit guides while doing demonstrations and seances. They are thought to be more advanced spirits or souls who, after their own earthly lives have ended, go into the next life (often called the spirit world) and become teachers to those that are less developed. Many guides are Native American because Native American peoples are spiritually advanced, aware of life after death and highly attuned to the natural world around them. For instance, the editor of *Psychic News* (the spiritualist newspaper) Maurice Barbanell, a medium himself, had his own Native American guide called Silver Birch, who often came through in circles to talk through him. Silver Birch became well known in the spiritualist movement as he, through Barbanell, wrote books on mediumship and spiritual topics. Of course, anyone who has evolved enough in spiritual terms to be able to help those slightly less developed has the potential to be a spirit guide.

So why did this spirit guide keep coming out of Jan's airing cupboard and how is it possible that she could see him? Most likely, she had some latent psychic abilities that enabled her to see the guide and the other spirits behind him. I believe the mist leaving her husband's body was his spirit leaving his earthly remains and that the cupboard was possibly a doorway to the next world, often called a portal. He passed away suddenly and may have been taken aback to realize that he still continued to exist beyond his physical body. He may have been trying to come back to communicate with his wife, but without any idea of how to contact her. Maybe the spirit guide agreed to help Jan's husband.

Taking a different point of view, the exhaustion arising from caring for her husband and then losing him could have caused Jan to have what is known as 'hypnagogic hallucinations', or incredibly vivid waking dreams that happen as someone drops off to sleep. However, Jan did report these visits happening around the same time each night. I think her subconscious mind was prompting her to wake regularly between 3am and 4am because the spirit world uses the unchallenging part of the mind to break through. She would have been alone in the same room as the portal, and the spirit guide was able to use the same 'doorway' as her late husband's spirit did. My belief is that Jan's husband was the second spirit, maybe accompanied by another family member. We don't know the outcome, but hopefully Jan did eventually manage to communicate with the spirit guide and her husband's spirit too. Some care workers have also witnessed strange mists leaving the bodies of the people they have been caring for as they died. Perhaps the actual act of caring and nurturing people as they draw close to death, opens up in many people that psychic sensitivity that enables them to witness such things.

THE POWER OF PORTALS

As shown by Jan's experience with a cupboard, many sightings of spirits seem to take place in doorways. In a recent television documentary about a haunted house in Scotland, the man living there said he often felt a very strong presence in the doorway behind him as he sat working at his computer. Later investigations with paranormal researchers in the show revealed high levels of electromagnetic energy around that particular doorway.

There are numerous reports of sightings that involve spirits appearing in doorways, or within some kind of framework like a hallway or a window setting. The British psychic medium and author Philip Kinsella arrived home one evening and saw his deceased friend standing in the entrance of his conservatory. Philip described his late friend as looking as though he was lit up around the edges of his body, with strands of light coming off him. He smiled, then vanished.

Mediums often use a cabinet structure in seance rooms when doing what is called 'physical mediumship', where a spirit takes on a solid form and may step out of the cabinet and walk around the room. Cabinets somehow contain the spirit energy before it is ready to be released into the room. (Today, many mediums actually use camping toilet tents as seance cabinets because they are light and portable, but no less effective!) Outside of a controlled seance, a spirit wishing to be seen may have to use whatever is available at hand to help concentrate its energy before it is released, as Jan's Native American spirit guide appeared to do.

I see the seance cabinet – or a cupboard, doorway, window and so on – as a makeshift portal that helps to channel spirit energy from one level or dimension of reality to another. Think of this like an oven. If you put a wet cake mixture inside the oven and leave the oven door open, the heat required to change the wet mixture into a solid form is leaking out. Closing the door contains the energy, in this case heat, and allows the cake to manifest. Like the oven, a seance cabinet enables psychic energy to build and intensify, so it can manifest spirits into our reality.

NATURE BEINGS

The next group of paranormal tales concern encounters with beings and spirits that appear to be closely connected to nature. The first of these comes from Jack Gale, an author who writes about magic and the paranormal. Jack recalled an odd experience his father had in the back garden of their London home in the mid-1950s. While he was down the end of the garden Jack's father observed his wife stepping out of the back door and walking towards him – and also saw that she was being followed by a 60 cm (2 ft) high creature covered in bark with twig-like appendages. It had a semi-transparent quality about it and appeared to sway in the breeze as it 'walked' behind Jack's mother, who didn't see or hear it herself. Although Jack's father never believed in anything of a paranormal nature, he was always adamant about seeing the twig-like figure and never changed his account.

We don't know if Jack's father was on some kind of medication that could have caused him to imagine this being. Perhaps sunlight or something in his eye made an ordinary plant blowing across the garden path, or even a nearby insect, appear larger. Jack himself believed what his father saw, and did not suggest he was in any way hallucinating. Stick insects, for example, tend to walk with a swaying kind of movement when walking across leaves. After all, plenty of images posted on social media illustrate how easy it is to play with perspective and show something that isn't real. On the other hand, if the creature was semi-transparent this could suggest it was not fully focused in our reality. Perhaps this type of creature normally inhabits the faerie realm and is a kind of fey. Some faeries are said to be protectors of nature. At the Findhorn Foundation in Scotland, the founders reported faeries helping the plants grow and looking after them. One faerie witness in Somerset saw two squirrels running up and down her aunt's tree in 2006, but they morphed into small human-like beings. She felt a telepathic type of communication from them, indicating that they were helping to look after the trees in the garden.

MOUSE FEY?

In 2010 Kate Ray, an artist, was walking down an old country track in Ashbury when she heard some noises coming from the hedge and saw slight movements. It felt rather odd to her, so she crept quietly towards the hedge and pulled aside some of the shrubbery so she could peer into it. There, she saw what she later described as a small creature – about the size of a human hand – with a body like a man's and wearing a pair of trousers but with a mouse-like face. It was standing upright, frozen to the spot and staring at her. After a few seconds it scurried away.

While this sounds like a creation from a Jim Henson muppets film or a Beatrix Potter book, Kate insisted that she had seen it and had not taken anything that might have caused her to dream or imagine the being. There are many examples of folkloric and religious beings with animal heads and human bodies: for example the ancient Egyptian god Set had a dog's head and Garuda, the Hindu god of strength, is often depicted with a bird's wings and beak. However, the hybrid creature in Kate's story is so unusual, my research found no other examples of creatures that were part man and part mouse. There is little other information to go on, other than it may possibly have been related to the faerie kingdom, but somehow shared characteristics with a mouse.

Kate herself speculated that the mouse-like appearance could have been a camouflage attempt in case it was spotted by humans. Maybe it was a shape-shifter, able to assume other forms depending on where it was – in this case, a rural hedge. But there is simply not enough information to attempt to classify it.

This wasn't Kate's only brush with the paranormal. While on a plane in 2011, she happened to look out the window, and saw what she described as a 'sky dragon': a large, twisting, snake-like creature in the sky. She watched it for some time as it flew alongside the plane at 30,000 ft (9,000 m). Wanting to check whether the passenger sitting beside her had also seen it, Kate looked across at him, but unfortunately he was fast asleep. Behind her seat another passenger was also looking out of the window. She asked him, 'Can you see that?' and he admitted that he too could see it, but after that said no more. She never got to speak to him after that, even after landing at the airport. It should be noted that some people are anxious flyers and it is possible for extreme anxiety to trick the mind. The idea of terrifying serpents or dragons isn't an unusual one, as these creatures appear in the mythology of cultures around the world, from the fearsome nine-headed ancient Greek Hydra to the life-creating rainbow serpent of Indigenous Australian peoples. But it is fascinating that two people appear to have seen this mysterious beast.

TREE SPIRITS

Spirits are often associated with humans and even animals, but some people also claim to have communicated with the spirits of trees. These beings are called 'dryads', from the Greek word for an oak tree. While the most famous dryad in Greek mythology is Daphne, who was transformed into a laurel tree to avoid capture by the god Apollo, it refers to any spirit or being that lives in a tree. Some legends suggest that the trees have souls or spirits, while others propose that spirits merge their consciousness with that of trees. Whatever the case, stories have emerged where people have interacted with trees and spirits associated with them in some way.

The *Seth Material* by the American author and medium Jane Roberts notes that if you pass a certain tree every day, it will in time learn to recognize your energy and will eventually be able to identify when you are coming. Every day, Gary May, an osteopath, would meditate and relax by his favourite oak tree in Canada without fail, spending up to an hour by the base of the tree. On one occasion, however, he could not get to 'his' tree due to work obligations. While at work, he felt a nagging feeling that he must down tools and get to the tree. He arrived to find his favourite tree had been chopped down, with just the stump now sticking out of the ground. Gary was shocked and heartbroken, but then he noticed a kind of glowing mist or cloud just above the stump and heard a voice that seemed to be coming from the strange mist. The voice thanked him for coming there every day and told him now it was time to say goodbye. With that, the mist faded into nothing. Presumably the tree's energy, or spirit, had gone.

Owls played an important role in many ancient cultures' mythologies.

Had the tree, over time, come to recognize Gary sitting beneath it and formed some kind of bond with him? It is interesting that this tree spirit felt the need to call out to Gary and say goodbye to him. If people felling trees felt this kind of kinship, the world would be a very different place! The next story suggests that it's not just trees that want to impart messages. Many legendary messengers have come in the form of animals – especially owls. Owls were viewed in different ancient cultures' mythologies as able to move between the mortal and spirit worlds. For example, Lilith, the ancient Sumerian goddess of death, has talons rather than feet.

WINGED MESSENGERS

Lyndon Gilchrist, a TV engineer from London, had, with other family members, some dream encounters with a half-owl and half-woman being. Initially, Lyndon recalled dreaming about an injured barn owl being swallowed up by a larger bird, then himself flying in the night sky with another owl over villages and towns. This dream happened shortly after his wife suffered a miscarriage. He felt his dream had a special meaning, and he had previously studied dreams as a source of help from the subconscious mind. For Lyndon, the injured barn owl could have represented the soul of a baby that was not capable of going through all the embryonic stages to birth. Therefore the soul abandoned the physical form and went back to where it might have come from. The larger bird swallowing the smaller one may have represented the soul returning to a group soul, or higher self as some might express it. According to Lyndon the later owl in his dream was a 'replacing soul' to come in, and their flight together in the night sky represented their shared future adventures on Earth.

Lyndon's wife Gina also saw a hybrid owl-human figure flying as fully formed waking visions through the bedroom and out of the window. Having researched this figure, they suspected it represented a pagan goddess called Hecate who was worshipped in ancient Greece (and possibly originated in Egypt or Anatolia in modern-day Turkey). Linked to the mysteries of life and death, in part her role was to take the souls of deceased children back to the spirit world where they came from. Obviously, given the loss of their child, this resonated strongly with the couple.

This 'new soul' arrived in the form of Lyndon's daughter, who was born a year later in August 1995 – curiously on the 'Day of Hecate', as celebrated in parts of Italy! During this time Lyndon and his wife were reminded of Hecate through a number of owl-related encounters. On the day of their daughter's birth, Lyndon had to go back to the delivery room on the floor below to collect some belongings. Walking down the stairs, rather than waiting for the lift, he passed a pregnant woman with her husband. Lyndon overheard the woman ask her husband, 'When are we going to visit your friend, who has the pet barn owl?' Lyndon stopped in his tracks.

A few days later, some friends came to visit the new arrival in the hospital, bringing a present for the baby. Lyndon unwrapped it carefully, to reveal a tiny candle carved into the shape of an owl. Both Lyndon and his wife were amazed at this choice of gift, considering their friends knew nothing of their owl experiences.

HECATE RETURNS

A few years later Lyndon and his wife told their daughter about seeing the owls around the time she was born. When the little girl was about four years old and the family were holidaying in Devon in south-west England, she told them she could see a figure in the trees who was half woman and half owl. 'Hecate was watching' her, she said, hiding behind Lyndon's legs in fear, and had 'scary eyes'. Later that evening, his wife suffered another miscarriage. Lyndon's daughter had no idea her mother was pregnant, and yet it seemed this strange visitor that took children had come once again to claim another. After this miscarriage the visitations and events related to owls and Hecate stopped for good.

They had one more child who was born by caesarean section, with no further miscarriages.

A sceptic might say that there was a confirmation bias at play in Lyndon and his wife seeing more owl symbols than usual; that they were looking out for these symbols because of their dreams, and as a way to help them cope with their loss. Older societies viewed messages in dreams as absolutely real calls to action or warnings from gods, angels or spirits in the afterlife. Today most psychologists would suggest that they are part of the unconscious mind. Perhaps the owl figure was created by Lyndon's and his family's minds as a joint experience. This suggest there is a vast subconscious mind that stirs beneath humanity. Carl Jung, the great psychoanalyst of the 20th century, proposed something of this nature and believed that dreams are highly important communications from other regions of our minds. Lyndon's dream of the owl may have been a highly symbolic pointer to a future event, but the next story shows such warnings can be more direct in nature.

DREAMS AS PROTECTION

In a dream, Paul Chaplin, a graphic designer, found himself in an airport departure lounge looking out of the terminal window, to see a passenger jet that was about to land. The plane was on fire and about to crash. He realized the danger everyone was in and tried to alert the other passengers in the terminal to clear the area.

Some three weeks later, in Paul's real life, he was in an American airport and had just gone through security checks and removed his boots to be scanned. He was busy putting his boots back on when he heard a man shout, 'Processing stop!' in a loud, commanding voice. All the security checking stopped and it was suddenly very quiet in the area.

After a minute or two of confusion and silence, with passengers including Paul wondering what was going on, four security staff came running through the area, looking worried. They ran to the terminal gate of a plane that had just landed and was about to release its passengers into the terminal. Around ten minutes later the security guards came back from the plane looking relieved. Paul asked one of them what was wrong, and was told that the plane that had just landed had actually been on fire as it parked beside the terminal building and they had gone to help! Luckily, no one was hurt and it was a small fire that they and the flight crew had quickly dealt with, but all the passengers of the plane were quickly evacuated as a precaution. Was this Paul's dream of three weeks earlier actually playing out?

It certainly seemed that his dream and the real-life event had similarities. In both, the plane was still on fire and even though Paul didn't see the plane actually land in his dream, the fire had started in the air. There was also a safety concern at the terminal in both events, albeit Paul was the one trying to evacuate people in the dream and the security staff did so in real life. But why did Paul dream this situation in particular?

Was Paul's subconscious mind trying to prove to him that it could show him the future, making sure to use an event in the near future and something so disturbing that he couldn't possibly ignore it? Maybe it was a message from some kind of higher self, or a protective angel-type being or spirit guide trying to warn him of potential danger ahead. If this was the case, it was arguably a strange choice to make, because it would be difficult for Paul to know how to make a positive contribution. Maybe, if the real-life situation had got worse, Paul would have been somehow prepared by his dream to encourage people to get out of the security area.

Higher selves are thought to be an aspect of the person's own soul, but a super part of their consciousness, that operates outside of space and time but can interact with the personality (the human experiencing life on Earth). Angels are sometimes thought to help in disasters or trying to prevent accidents. Claire Millins in 2023 was driving to Lincoln on the left-hand side of the road (the correct side). However, she heard a voice in the car suddenly telling her to steer the car into the right-hand lane. It repeated itself when Claire didn't do it. Because Claire believed that she was somehow receiving guidance, she acted upon the voice and steered the car into the right-hand lane. Just at that moment, another car on the wrong side of the road came round the corner of the bend. Had Claire not moved to the right-hand side, the oncoming car would have hit hers, possibly resulting in serious injury or death. Had an angel or spirit guide intervened and saved her life?

Carl Jung believed that prophetic dreams were manifestations of the unconscious mind. He believed dreams had a transformative power in self-discovery and personal growth and could provide important messages. Jung believed that God speaks chiefly through dreams and visions, and by listening to dreams, it was possible to avert disasters.

DREAMS OF ROGUE NEW WORLDS

In 1991 Paul had another dream that was so extraordinary he can recall much of it today and calls it his 'spiritual time travel dream' because it contained elements from different time periods. In the dream, he found himself in the audience of a theatre, watching a stage performance of the BBC TV series *Dr Who*. In this instance he was watching the fourth incarnation of The Doctor, played by the actor Tom Baker, complete with his floppy hat and long scarf.

While watching the performance, Paul glanced briefly to his left and noticed that the brilliant Victorian science fiction author H.G. Wells was sitting in the same row as himself, also watching the play. Paul wanted to say hello and show Wells his digital watch, as he thought the modern timepiece would interest him. He made his way over and without even saying hello, held out his wrist and showed Wells the digital display on the watch, saying something like, 'Look what we have in my time.' Wells took out a pocket watch typical of his era and said, 'Well, look at this.' However, this was no ordinary pocket watch, and when Wells opened it up, the timepiece projected a sort of hologram showing the entire solar system. This virtual schematic clearly showed the arrangement of celestial bodies in our solar system. But it also showed another larger planet moving in between the orbits of Earth and Mars: the name 'Archon' was clearly printed on this planet, together with the year '2034' or possibly '2036' just above it. So the dream seemed to suggest that in Paul's lifetime a new planet might enter our solar system.

Suddenly, the dream changed, and Paul was now in the future, either 2034 or 2036, looking up into the sky at a planet that was larger than our moon. An old man alongside Paul explained that this planet (Archon) was now causing havoc on Earth by altering the gravitational forces affecting our home planet. Paul wondered if nuclear missiles could be fired at it, but the old man said everything had been tried and nothing was working. Paul remembered a feeling of great fear and distress in this part of the dream, and then the dream ended.

It is interesting that the dream showed a huge planet, big enough to pull Earth out of the 'Goldilocks zone', which has just the right temperature to sustain life. Does this mean that Paul's dream is predicting a future catastrophe for Earth, and maybe the end of humanity, just as dinosaurs were wiped out millions of years ago, probably as the result of an asteroid strike? Could this dream have been a warning from the spirit world?

Paul himself said he doesn't know how to think about it. Even if it was some kind of warning from another dimension about a future apocalypse, there is little that one person could do about it. However, it's interesting that in 2015 Nasa explained that US scientists had found mathematical evidence for a hypothetical Planet X (nicknamed 'Planet 9') located in the far reaches of the solar system beyond Pluto. Signs of this unproven planet, supposedly ten times the size of Earth, apparently included a slight 'wobble' in the orbit of a remote ring of space debris called the Kuiper Belt. Paul's unsettling dream, remember, occurred many years before this!

Mythical planets such as Nibiru were also thought to come into our orbit long ago and visitors from that planet seeded the creation of humankind on to Earth as it slowly passed by. The idea of Nibiru comes from the writings of researcher Zecharia Sitchin, who studied the legends of the Sumerian civilization that existed around c.4100 to 1750 BCE, around Mesopotamia, in present day Iraq. In their own creation

Paul encountered H.G. Wells in a dream that he described as an instance of 'spiritual time travel'.

legends, the Sumerians described how the Gods created mankind and came from another planet they called Nibiru, which had a 35,000-year orbit around the Sun. The gods/Nibirunians wanted to mine gold from Earth as they passed close to our orbit. But after some time, they decided that it was better to create slaves to do the job for them. Sitchin believed it was their intervention that seeded humans on Earth through DNA manipulation with other early hominids of Earth at the time, such as the Neanderthal man. The bottom line was that man came from a cross between the gods and the dominant species on our planet at the time, the Neanderthals.

Could Paul's dream be anything to do with those ideas? Maybe the two might be connected with his dream and the mythical stories of this planet both pointing towards the same outcome. Only time will tell.

While all the experiences recounted so far are extraordinary, they mostly reflect the fact that many people all over the world claim to have encountered magical otherworldly beings and spirits, and had strangely prophetic dreams. Some paranormal stories, however, are so bizarre they almost defy any kind of categorization.

GIANT GODDESS

Owen Simons, a security guard, who in 1995 was living on the Caribbean island of Saint Lucia, did not believe in 'ghosties, ghoulies and things that go bump in the night', as he put it. Owen and his friend used to walk home together after visiting a local bar. On each occasion they would walk up the hill and past the church before heading off to their respective homes. One night, while walking up the hill to the church, they both noticed a large shape over the roof of the church. It was a giant woman sitting astride the roof, with her feet over either side of the walls! She was at least 50 feet tall, with long white flowing hair, very pale white skin, and wearing long flowing robes. She looked, as Owen put it, 'as white as that fridge'. Owen asked his friend, who by now was cowering in fright behind a gravestone, if he saw it too. His buddy nodded, obviously terrified, but it was enough to confirm to Owen that they both saw her.

Being the braver of the two, Owen stood his ground and decided to pick up a stone and throw it at this huge woman perched on the roof. The giant did not take kindly to this, he said. She stood up, stepped off the church and started to walk towards them both. As she got closer, though, she began to diminish in size, eventually becoming the height of a normal human being. But she also started to slowly sink into the ground as she walked towards them and eventually vanished, as if she was disappearing into quicksand. Bewildered at what they just experienced, both men went home in shock.

Now both men had been drinking that evening, but alcohol isn't known for inducing visual hallucinations. They experienced the same thing and both took logical action out of fear, either hiding behind the gravestone or challenging and testing it by throwing the stone to see if it was real. Nor did Owen say he had taken any kind of drug before this encounter, which would cause him to doubt the experience.

What could this encounter be? In his 1996 book *Goddesses, Guardians and Groves*, Jack Gale, the author whose father had the strange encounter with the twig-like being, wrote that as Christianity subsumed ancient pagan religions, churches would often be built over much older sacred sites or ley lines (connections between such sites that form a kind of earth energy grid). He noted that many areas would attract the protection of energies or act as a focal point for energies that he interpreted as protectors or guardians of the sites in question. Often, he said, these would be in the form of goddess-like creatures, with female energies perhaps acting as protectors of portals, to stop certain things coming through into our world. These would be supernatural and spiritual super-humans. Hecate from Greek legend is one such goddess or luminary being who was thought to protect households, boarders and cities, and acted between one realm or sphere and the next, protecting people from intruders into our world. As such, traditional spirit guides in seances perform similar roles in temporal setups in a seance room.

BLUE GLOWING VISITORS

In the early 1970s Dave Monks was a junior staff member in a laboratory that researched high-tech electronics as part of its defence-based work for the UK government. His special focus was on development of the microchip (the 'brain' that today drives millions of smartphones, computers and other electronic devices). The laboratory was based inside a large old manor house in the English countryside, used as the company's business premises, possibly identified as the now defunct Rudlow Manor.

One day, Dave was at his station, across from a colleague on the opposite side of the room, both focusing intently upon their electronics work. Suddenly they were distracted by a bright blue light illuminating the room, and looked up to see a blue glowing box, approximately the size of a shoebox, floating down the middle of the room between them. It moved with absolute silence. They watched in astonishment as the blue box glided silently past them and out through an open door, turning right down a corridor and going out of their view.

After gathering themselves and confirming with each other that they had both seen it, they went to find their supervisor and explained as best they could what they had both witnessed, not entirely sure if the supervisor would actually believe them. The supervisor listened with interest and then said, 'Follow me.' He took them down to an area in the basement of the old manor house where a long-time employee was working and asked the two men to repeat their experience with the blue box to this older colleague. The man nodded his head and then said that he too had seen this strange box on previous occasions.

Some time later, during the 1980s, a similar story began circulating among the UFO community. Again, it happened at an establishment doing work for the UK's Ministry of Defence. The tale was leaked by a whistleblowing employee, who said that one night, a security guard patrolling the building had seen a blue light emanating from behind the frosted window in one locked door. He unlocked it, cautiously opened the door and shone his torch in.

A SECOND STRANGE VISITOR

He was confronted by the figure of a man wearing some kind of helmet that was glowing bright blue. The blue light filled the room and was so bright that the guard could clearly see the man was in front of an open filing cabinet, rifling through the folders inside. The strange helmeted figure turned around, saw the startled security guard and instantly vanished in front of his eyes! The security guard managed to raise the alarm and the next day the whole building was filled with security personnel, including government intelligence officers, investigating the incident. The poor security guard was reported to be so traumatized he needed psychiatric treatment in hospital. The whistleblower also claimed that she overheard her boss in the next room the following morning being interviewed by investigators, and saying, 'Whatever we try and do, we cannot stop them getting in!'

Who – or what – were the 'them' he was referring to, and was this incident linked to that of the box, which also glowed blue? In this case I tend to think the blue glowing box was some kind of reconnaissance device. The fact that it had already been seen on previous occasions, did not fit the general description of a ghost or spirit, and appeared to be searching in a location known for highly sensitive research and possibly secret spy technology, suggests there was a specific purpose and intelligence behind it. It's plausible to think the blue box could have been a remotely controlled device on a search-and-identify mission. Today, we are well aware of the flying drones that are often used in warfare and surveillance. These remotely controlled aircraft and small helicopters can inspect areas unsafe for humans and are a cheaper and safer alternative for military missions than traditional aircraft manned by humans. They employ the physics of aeronautics, using the air under wings to lift the craft up. They do, however, create noise as they fly, unlike the blue box, which flew silently. On the other hand, the blue box incidents occurred around 50 years ago, and it is surprising that since then no information has emerged that even comes close to the description of that technology.

As for the mysterious helmeted man who vanished, again it is possible that an unfriendly government could have developed some kind of cloaking technology using blue light, which the mysterious visitor was able to use. The box did not seem to be 'bothered' by the fact that it was sighted on this occasion or previous occasions, almost as if it had no fear of being caught, maybe because it could also somehow dematerialize or self-destruct in that situation. What we can reasonably assume is that the secret technology being researched and developed at this laboratory was probably the reason this device was floating around and gathering information.

Let's also consider some of the possible paranormal explanations. Blue lights have been described in many UFO sightings. It may have resulted from their exotic propulsion systems or perhaps their protective shielding. A recent UFO sighting from a video of April 2024 in the desert city of Scottsdale, near Phoenix, Arizona, seems to show a blue UFO appearing to come out of nowhere and hover across the city. Many contactees and abductees who claim to have been taken aboard craft by extra-terrestrials mention that the beings on them seem to be highly telepathic in nature, so the blue box devices could be alien technology that gathers human knowledge directly from individuals' brainwaves as it glides past them. However, it would only be able to gather mental information if the persons it was scanning knew that information, and much defence-related work is done on a need-to-know basis. This could explain why the strange visitor in the blue light-emitting helmet was going through filing cabinets looking for information that was written down.

SPIRIT OR ALIEN?

Perhaps the two incidents are linked and the intelligence behind the box is the same as the one behind the strange visitor with the helmet. The helmeted visitor had the extra ability of being able to dematerialize at will. What is also interesting is that would mean he possessed the same physical abilities as those attributed to seance spirits, where the spirits are able to materialize in the seance room at will, given the right conditions. (For more on this, see Chapter 4.) And, of course, the remark that 'they cannot be stopped' would make sense in this case. Is it also feasible that the helmeted visitor came out of the filing cabinet, using the cabinet rather like a portal, as a seance cabinet is used by a psychic medium? Perhaps the helmet was there to protect him not so much from our atmosphere, but from the effects of the blue light itself, which might be too bright when someone or something is in very close proximity to it or even generating it.

I believe there are many more instances of this type that have occurred at research establishments, where all manner of secret and groundbreaking technology is developed. Beings that are higher up the scale of technological evolution, which could include extra-terrestrial beings or even those from other dimensions, could be 'dropping in' to keep an eye on the scientific and technological advances humans are making, maybe concerned that it might in some way affect them or their intentions. Therefore the phrase 'extra-dimensional beings' conjures up the intriguing idea that not only could there be faerie beings, ghosts and spirits watching us closely, but also alien boxes, helmeted beings and myriad other mysterious entities that cannot even be classified!

CHAPTER TWO

HOSPITALIZED SPIRITS, PSYCHIC DOCTORS AND LIFE-SAVERS

Many believers in the paranormal say that at the moment of our death we become 'discarnate' – that is, our physical being dies but our consciousness continues. It is then able to move into the spirit world, where it can evolve into a higher and purer energy. Spirits are entities that move into the light of that world after earthly death. Ghosts are different in that they appear on Earth but do not interact with the living as a spirit may do if it returns to Earth. Ghosts can be seen as a type of recorded energy on the atmosphere, which can be picked up by psychics or mediums, or perhaps they are bleed-throughs of life forms from other times. Their energy replays their final moments on Earth or some particular trauma or emotional event. The next chapter will explore the subject of ghosts and memory imprints in more detail.

You have probably seen ghost hunting teams on television shows about the paranormal visiting graveyards and scanning the area with electromagnetic meters in the hope of finding spirits of the dead. However, the evidence in this chapter suggests that we are more likely to find those who have recently left their earthly bodies in the places where they died, rather than where their bodies are later buried. As shown in these accounts, a hospital, the scene of a disaster, or the person's home can all be places where the recently dead are still, in some form, present.

For most people the transition to the next world, whatever that world may be, seems to be straightforward. But not every death is an easy passing. Many fascinating experiences have been reported in hospitals or on the way to them, where medical staff have witnessed a patient (or someone else) in their afterlife. We will also discover how some of these entities can be sighted in mirrors and how, in desperate situations, people on this side of life and the next help each other.

HOSPITAL 'HAUNTINGS'

Perhaps it is not surprising that so many paranormal events are reported in hospitals. After all, many people are seriously ill or injured before they die, and will pass on either in a hospital or on the way to one. Many medical professionals have had experiences where they have seen or felt the spirits of newly deceased patients around them at the hospitals they work in. In fact, some nursing training in certain UK hospitals now involves an aspect of spiritualism. If a nurse comes off shift but feels a presence around them which could be that of a deceased patient they have been looking after, they have been advised to return to the hospital to have it 'dealt with'.

The stories in the following pages can be seen as evidence that some spirits of the newly dead do not always go straight on to the spirit realm after leaving their corporeal residence. A medium might explain that when someone dies, in most cases they progress to a higher spiritual plane (that many call Heaven, the spirit world or the other side). Those that pass over are not cleansed or perfect in any way, but often assisted to cross over by those on the other side of life. Once there, they begin to acclimatize to their new environment, where the energies of the Earth plane have less effect on them, and a kind of healing will often take place. However, some do not immediately make this crossover journey, which can be for a variety of reasons, some known and some not. Some do not believe that such an afterlife exists, and their beliefs may temporally trap them here on earth. Others die in a state of shock and their minds are confused as to why they cannot be heard or seen by those they left behind. They are often stuck on the Earth plane until they get another opportunity to move on, or are helped by a medium, a deceased family member or friend or even a spirit guide.

SPIRIT AMBULANCE

Dave White, a vehicle breakdown and recovery worker, was interested in the paranormal and in his spare time he and his girlfriend investigated haunted places as a hobby. However, it was in his day job that he had the most haunting of encounters! Dave's work involved helping stranded motorists to get going again in their cars and vans, and also recovering broken-down ambulances. If an ambulance needed repairing but could still be driven, he would have to drive it back to the depot to be fixed. On one occasion Dave was called to collect an ambulance that had been damaged in a minor collision. He jumped into the driver's seat and as he adjusted the side mirror his heart skipped a beat. In the mirror he saw a woman sitting in the back of the ambulance, looking back at him.

Dave turned around in his seat to look directly at the back of the ambulance – but no physical person was there. Alone in the cab and suddenly feeling very on edge, Dave looked in the wing mirror again and realized he could still see the woman sitting in the back. Even though he was a hobbyist ghost hunter this experience unnerved Dave so much, he decided to phone his girlfriend. She answered and suggested, 'Why don't you ask the woman questions?' While this seemed a reasonable enough request, Dave told his girlfriend that he did not want to because he was alone; he said that if another person was with him in the cab, he might have felt confident enough to approach the unknown dweller in the back of the ambulance. After a while the image of the woman faded away into nothing in the mirror and Dave drove the ambulance back to the depot without further incident.

What could have happened in this case? As she appeared in an ambulance, it seems likely the woman was taken ill or was dying and was on her way to hospital for emergency care but didn't survive the journey and was declared dead on arrival. Emergency medical staff at the hospital would have recorded this and her lifeless body would have been transferred to a hospital mortuary, before being removed for burial or cremation by a funeral director. Maybe the woman had no belief in the afterlife or simply didn't give it much thought in her daily life, so when she died it was not a natural process straight away for her to pass on to the next phase of existence.

Dave White discovered a mysterious figure sitting in the back of an ambulance while taking it back for repairs.

If it is the case that some souls leaving this world have some difficulties passing into the spirit realm, I think most of their problems stem from where the person dies and also their mental state as they pass over. A lot of people leave this world confused about what is happening, simply because they have no belief or understanding of an afterlife. If you do believe, or at least have some open-minded opinions about it, then you adjust a lot better to your new surroundings. It is possible that the woman's essence remained inside the ambulance – or that even an imprint of it remained there, like a memory recording.

TRAPPED BY THE AMBULANCE?

Another idea that could explain this experience is that the ambulance itself might have been acting rather like a physical medium's seance or spirit cabinet: an enclosed box-like container that a certain type of medium uses to help spirits become visible to those who are not psychically inclined to see them. During a seance, spirits that are about to appear manifest inside the contained structure of the cabinet, using the material called ectoplasm. This opaque, viscous substance allows 'ordinary' people to see the spirit as their previous earthly self, and allows them to be touched or maybe even measured. Ectoplasm is taken from the medium, who generates it from energy points (chakras) in their own body, such as the solar plexus.

When the cabinet door is opened (or sometimes a curtain is lifted) the materialized spirit is able to release its energy, be seen as a solid being and move about the room for a limited time. My theory is that perhaps the ambulance, being a box-like structure itself, had somehow trapped the spirit for a while until it could hopefully be released or collected later by a more experienced soul acting as a spirit guide. It is interesting that this spirit did not appear to Dave using an using ectoplasmic form; instead, he saw her as a reflection in the ambulance's side mirror. This entity may have been appearing as its 'etheric' or 'astral' self, in which case it could only have been seen by psychically sensitive people – like Dave, who is obviously attuned to the spirit world. The etheric body is essentially the spirit of the deceased person but not a materialization of the physical body. The etheric body can be thought of as the first phase of spiritual existence, as a form the spirit takes, but is closer to our world.

GHOSTLY 'REFLECTIONS'

A spirit appearing in a mirror is not an uncommon phenomenon. Mediums have long noticed that spirits can be perceived with mirrors by those sensitive enough to see them. Indeed, the ancient Egyptians used 'scrying mirrors' to try to communicate with the dead. The 16th-century prophet Nostradamus also employed the 'scrying' method, in his case gazing into a still bowl of water to achieve a trance state that would allow him to foretell the future.

You may remember Owen Simons, who had already encountered a bizarre goddess-like giant (see Chapter 1). He went on to have another strange experience, this time involving an apparition that he saw in a mirror. In 1998, he was driving down a road in Middlesex, England, when he looked in his rear-view mirror and suddenly saw a woman sitting in the back seat of his car. The shock of seeing this apparition made Owen put his foot down on the accelerator; he ended up breaking the speed limit and was pulled over to the side of the road by a police vehicle. He apologized to the police officer and explained that it happened because he had seen a phantom in the back of his car.

While you might assume this would have carried little weight with law enforcement, in fact the police officer simply advised Owen to drive home without even issuing him with a ticket for speeding! Owen got the distinct impression that the officer was aware a strange woman had been appearing in cars along that stretch of road. There are all kinds of reports from around the world where different motorists have spotted what seems to be the same ghostly figure, and even interacted with it, on the same section of highway. A car leasing company published the results of a poll on its website of how many reports of ghosts or spirits are seen in different areas of the UK roads. The poll found 36 per cent of people in the Greater London area thought they'd seen a road ghost or spirit at some point in their lives, compared with 15 per cent of respondents in Scotland and 14 per cent in north-west England.

A sceptic might counter that the policeman was being generous simply because he was busy or maybe at the end of his shift, and there were no aggravating factors involved, like drink or drugs. It should be noted that staring into a mirror for a long time can induce a visual illusion called the 'Troxler effect', where an image can blur and disappear, and that Dave noted the woman faded away after a while. But, as he then reported, she did reappear in the mirror.

What about paranormal events inside a hospital building itself? It's not difficult to imagine that strange events such as the ones that follow could be related somehow to the heightened pain, joy, fear and loss that happen every day in the hospital setting.

A RELUCTANT END OF LIFE?

Abbie Stone was working as a nurse in a hospital in south-west England in 2017. She nursed in an area known as the 'end of life' ward, where patients who are nearing death receive palliative care. The ward is designed to be a place of quiet and calm to help the patients pass away as peacefully as possible. Abbie was asked by one of her patients during the night for some more pillows to make her more comfortable. She went out and into a deserted corridor with storage rooms on one side and on the opposite side empty rooms where empty beds had been made up in case any new patients arrived.

As she entered a storage room, Abbie heard a strange sound coming from an empty room across the corridor. She went over to that room and peered in but saw nothing out of the ordinary, just a made-up bed and a small table next to it. She turned her attention back to the storage cupboard and fetched the pillows from a cupboard, which took no more than a few seconds. Hearing a noise, she left this room and once again looked into the room across the hall, where the noise was coming from.

This time, she saw that the previously made-up bed now had its covers thrown off and the small table by the bed was now across the room and by the window. Something or someone had moved the covers and table, even though there was no one in sight and everything was now quiet. Abbie was taken aback by this, but thought there must be a rational explanation. She returned to the end of life ward and spoke to her colleague on the reception desk, who insisted that no one else was in that part of the hospital.

One potential explanation for Abbie's experience is a poltergeist type of phenomena might have occurred in the room. A poltergeist, from the German for 'noisy spirit', is a kind of afterlife entity or force whose activities are often violent and malicious and can be highly unpredictable. Given that Abbie saw no one else in the area who could have moved the items, it might be that the concentration of people near or at death in the end of life ward was somehow responsible for the disturbances that Abbie witnessed. It's possible that the mind of a newly deceased person is highly confused because staff and other patients they have got to know can suddenly no longer see them. Might they wander around the hospital, frustrated, the energy they throw off pushing around smaller items like chairs, tables or bed covers?

THE SPIRIT WORKMAN

In 2018 at the same hospital, renovation work was being carried out to upgrade one of the wards from Monday to Friday, and during the weekend the ward was empty. A nurse called Tina Warden had come into the ward during the weekend to deal with medicines that had to be organized during the refurbishment. To her surprise, she saw what she thought was a workman in his overalls, wearing something like a miner's helmet or safety hat. The man did not respond to any of Tina's greetings; he simply walked into an alcove at the end of the ward and vanished into it. Tina went over to the alcove and tried to find him but he was no longer there. There was no other way out, other than walking in the direction where Tina had come from. Tina was not aware of there being any accidents with workmen in the past at the hospital, so the mystery remained as to who he might have been.

ALERTED TO A YOUNG SOUL IN PAIN

Nurse Carrie Kirkwall reported a strange incident that occurred at the high-dependency ward of a different hospital on the south-west coast of England. Where she worked, seriously ill people were connected to life support machines and using oxygen masks to breathe. When a patient 'crashed' (suffered a cardiac arrest) the doctors on the floor above, along with supporting medical staff, would get an emergency pager bleep alerting them to the fact that a patient needed urgent medical attention. They didn't usually take the lift as it was too slow for speedy access to the high-dependency ward below, and would just run down two flights of stairs to get there as quickly as possible.

On one occasion in 2010 their pagers started bleeping and the on-duty senior doctor and his two junior doctors ran down the first flight of stairs. They began to run down the second flight when they were suddenly halted in their tracks, nearly tripping over a young female patient who was sitting hunched over on one of the steps. The senior doctor asked this girl why she was sitting there and not in her bed? The girl was also rocking backwards and forwards and kept saying her stomach hurt so much. The doctor told her to stay put and that they would get someone to help her, but first they had to go and help another patient who was very sick.

The medics carried on down the stairs and into the high-dependency ward, where another staff member told them that it was too late and the crash patient was already clinically dead. Going over to make absolutely sure they couldn't revive the patient, they were shocked to see it was the girl they had met on the stairs. They tried to resuscitate her, but to no avail. Not quite believing what they were seeing, they sent another staff member to see if the girl was still sitting on the staircase, but that person reported back that there was now no one there.

So what could have happened? One explanation is that the doctors were rushing to an emergency and the young cardiac arrest patient just happened to look similar to the girl on the stairs. But these were medical professionals used to dealing with high-pressure situations, which in my opinion suggests the girl on the stairs was the spirit of the girl who had just died in the ward. But why would she be sitting on the staircase and why, if she was now out of her body, would she be in so much pain? Recalling the female apparition in the ambulance, who may have been temporarily trapped inside it, it's possible that the staircase could have acted in a similar way. After passing over, the girl's spirit may have floated upwards out of her body and her soul or energy became trapped in the stairway until she could be helped to the next level. (Stairs in hospital buildings typically have doors that are kept closed for fire safety reasons.) It's my view that her soul or spirit was temporarily operating in our system of reality so that she could be seen by the doctors and talk to them. As for the pain she was suffering, again it could be that as she was still operating on our physical level to some extent, so her spirit consciousness may have continued to feel the pain of the earthly world.

ASTRAL TRAVEL

Another paranormal explanation for this strange experience relates to the 'astral cord', described by some occultists and spiritualists as a spiritual version of the umbilical cord that connects a mother and baby in the womb. The astral cord connects the spirit to the human body through the solar plexus, the mid-section of the body where the navel is situated. People who practise astral travel enable their soul or spirit to temporarily leave their body while in a sleep or trance state so it can wander elsewhere. Their astral cord maintains the connection with the body and helps bring them back to it after they have travelled, rather like a ship's anchor. The cord is supposed to stretch and it only breaks when death of the body occurs, allowing the spirit to permanently leave the body.

As the girl on the stairs was complaining of her stomach hurting, perhaps her astral cord had broken or snapped and this pain of it snapping, while not physical, was distressing for her. However, it was pain in her mind or consciousness. She was still somehow in our reality, albeit temporarily, and therefore still attuned to its hurts and ills, but as soon as she left it the distress and pain would no longer be felt. Given that nobody was on the stairs when the staff member went to check, I suspect that a guide or loved one in spirit came to collect her and take her soul on to the spirit world. For more on astral travelling and out-of-body experiences, Robert Monroe's *Journeys Out of the Body* is a classic in its field.

Anyone who takes an open-minded approach to the paranormal can see that, speaking purely statistically, some medical professionals are likely to be psychic, often without realizing it. A small percentage do, however, become aware that they have an ability to communicate with departed souls.

THE PSYCHIC DOCTOR

In the early 2000s Dr Ian Rubenstein was a general practitioner at his busy medical practice in Enfield in north London, dealing with a wide range of medical issues. (His patient lists actually included some of the original witnesss to the famous 'Enfield poltergeist' case, which occurred in a house in the area in the 1970s.) Ian has other, more unusual skills in addition to his medical knowledge: namely, a talent for communication with spirits. In 1974, as a young medical student of 19, he had his first experience of transfiguration, a process often involving a medium where an otherworldly or discarnate being projects their spirit face over the face of a medium or sometimes an ordinary person who is in the room.

In this case Ian was with his younger sister and a group of friends at a house. One friend, a dark-haired teenager called Felicity, had a crush on Ian at the time that he was aware of and he admitted that he played around with her feelings a little bit. As the friends were hanging out, without warning Felicity's face suddenly changed into what Ian described as something like the Snow Queen from *The Lion, the Witch and the Wardrobe*. He said her face now looked extremely white, with high cheekbones, piercing blue eyes and blue, frosty-looking lips. Also, her hair was now blonde and shoulder length. Ian's sister, sitting to the side of Felicity, also noticed this sudden transfiguration and screamed in shock, jumping out of her chair.

Then things turned even stranger as the mysterious face spoke through the young girl. The voice was forceful, as if used to commanding respect, and said, 'Stop! Keep back. What you are doing is wrong!' Ian understood this to mean he should stop flirting with Felicity, as he was causing her emotional turmoil. Then the voice said, 'Mark this, know there is more to life than meets the eye and then one day you will understand.' By now Ian's sister was shouting, 'My god, can you see those lips?' Ian looked at his sister to be sure they had both witnessed the same thing. He turned back to face the 'Snow Queen' but Felicity's face had now returned to normal.

Later in his life, Ian would see demonstrations of transfiguration at spiritualist churches but he commented that, 'All those demonstrations just never cut it, whereas this experience was a jaw-dropping moment, in your face and without question very real indeed!' He was thankful that his sister had also witnessed it, which confirmed that neither was having some kind of hallucination or even a mental health breakdown. Later, experienced mediums explained to Ian that this must have been the girl's spirit guide coming through and using the opportunity to reach out to Ian. Transfigurations are not always seen by everyone in the room: more often, they are seen by those who are tuned in to the spirit world. It appears that Ian and his sister somehow tuned in to Felicity's spirit guide without realizing it. Ian would go on to develop his own mediumistic skills and use them to help his patients in a psychical way as well as treating them medically.

SPIRIT CONSULTATIONS

Initially Ian focused on his medical career, preferring a purely scientific approach to understanding the universe and life. But after a friend encouraged him to attend an open psychic development circle in Walthamstow, north London, he began to learn the ropes of spirit communication and mediumship. This suggests to me that the spirit world had plans for Ian.

He said that as someone who had been taught to study and analyze things, he found this all rather strange. Random messages and images would be placed in his mind by spirit communicators and he would just have to relay these to strangers in the circle. Often he had no idea what the messages meant, but they seemed to be meaningful to the other circle members. He grew more confident over time that there really was something paranormal going on because of the way the messages were making sense to the recipients. Then, said Ian, he began getting communications from the spirit world coming through while he was at work.

In 2008 a patient named Lucy came into Ian's surgery in tears and despite his best efforts to calm her and get to the bottom of her distress, she couldn't explain it and just continued weeping inconsolably. He decided the best he could do for her for the time being was to prescribe some antidepressants. As the prescription was being printed off, Ian felt a blow to his head. He then felt a presence behind him which he perceived telepathically as saying, 'Ask her about her father,' and he saw the misty outline of a man forming over Lucy's left shoulder. Ian said, 'Lucy, tell me about your father.' She was so surprised she was able to stop crying and explain that her father died 38 years earlier in awful circumstances, in Northern Ireland. He had been quite a vocal critic of the IRA (Irish Republican Army) and he was later found dead in a ditch, having been tarred and feathered and 'kneecapped', or shot in the knees. It was thought the IRA was responsible for his death. Lucy said in two days' time it would be the anniversary of his passing.

Ian described the figure who was standing by Lucy's shoulder and asked if his description resembled her father. Lucy told him the description did indeed sound very much like him. She jumped up, held Ian by his arm and when he handed the prescription to her she said, 'Thank you but I don't need these now!' Word soon spread about Dr Rubenstein's psychic abilities, and often patients would come out after having had an appointment with him and complain to the receptionist if he did not give them a reading at the same time! While Ian's later connection with the spirit world came about through his mediumship, others in the medical world may have continued their practice after passing over into the next life.

SPIRITUAL SURGERY

George Chapman was working as a fireman in the 1950s but in his spare time he claimed to channel the spirit of a deceased eye surgeon named Dr William Lang, who worked at the famous Moorfields Eye Hospital in London. Such a doctor did actually exist and died in 1937.

George became interested in spiritualism after the premature death of his four-week-old daughter.

He was introduced to the paranormal by a colleague at the fire brigade who owned a Ouija board. He said he received messages through this board from his daughter, even though she was just an infant when she died so would not have been able to spell out words. George was convinced that she had informed him that she was now growing up on the other side. Later, he said, other spirits came through the board and informed him that he would develop into a spiritual healer.

Eventually, George began to do psychic operations on patients. Or rather, after George went into a trance the spirit of Dr Lang emerged and lifted the spirit body out of the patient. An entranced George would then move his hands above the physical body, appearing to perform complex spiritual 'operations' that could not be seen by the human eye. Dr Lang claimed he was helped in these procedures by his own deceased son, and other doctors in the spirit world. They even had a deceased secretary who would keep accurate records on the other side for patients who were treated!

Many successful treatments were reported by patients, including some treatments of patients who were seen as children by Dr Lang

The renowned Moorfields Eye Hospital, where George Chapman worked and supposedly channelled the spirit of Dr William Lang.

during his own lifetime. The patients were treated for a whole variety of conditions, not just eye-related issues. Now as adults they heard about George Chapman channelling Dr Lang and so decided to come back to their trusted surgeon for further treatment of their health conditions. Some patients reported that they were successfully treated second time around, through spirit intervention. Spiritual healing would be done at a different level than physical treatments, because Dr Lang was manipulating the energies of the spirit body. These often had greater success than any physical healing, and Dr Lang could accomplish more on his patients from his spiritually based operations.

When Dr Lang's own daughter Marie Lyndon Lang heard about George Chapman's claims she, after some hesitation, eventually agreed to George visiting her to demonstrate his claim that her father continued to live beyond his physical death and was also treating people from his side of life. At first she dismissed him, but eventually he gave her so much compelling evidence that she became convinced George was actually channelling her father through his trance mediumship. Marie hosted George at her house every month for another 30 years. During these visits she would listen as her father came through in spirit and advised other doctors about problems they needed help with.

Marie later wrote a published letter which confirmed that it was her father coming through George Chapman. In a second letter to be opened after death, she again verified George as genuine and said her late father was speaking through him while he was in a trance. The letter also mentioned the names of the doctors who attended the private trance sessions and witnessed 'Dr Lang' talking through George. However, these names were never revealed to the public. George apparently felt that this knowledge might publicly embarrass them, or any of their family members who were also in the medical profession. He later passed on in 2006 and his son Michael continues to work as a spiritual healer in Wales.

Was George Chapman some kind of psychic 'scalpel' for Dr William Lang? Dr Lang's daughter obviously believed he was. While we cannot know for sure, open-minded enquiry should not ignore that some of those who claim psychic abilities may be seeking to take advantage of vulnerable people. True mediums and spiritualists often feel a driving need to help and heal. And just like doctors and nurses – whether in our reality or in the spirit world – their special abilities mean they are always on call. Some even act as a kind of psychic emergency service, as demonstrated in the stories below.

THE GIRL ON THE FERRY

When disasters such as earthquakes occur or wars break out, people die suddenly and often in a state of shock. Their passing is typically not peaceful and, as previously mentioned, their soul or spirit can get temporarily stuck in this world, although they may remain unseen by those who are still living. Glasgow-based medium Ian Shanes had a heartbreaking experience that involved him helping a spirit to cross over. One night in 1987 he suddenly found himself out of his body and in deep water, inside a large ship that was still floating but had capsized on to its side. He saw a small girl who was crying and holding a teddy bear, sitting on the side of a staircase that had turned over along with the ship. Ian instinctively knew he was there to help her. He asked her where her mummy and daddy were but she said she did not know, so he promised to help her find her them.

Ian sent out a request mentally for help and suddenly saw a kind of hatch or portal opening up above the girl in what was now the ceiling (although it was actually the side of the capsized ship). Ian lifted the small girl up, saying, 'Go up there and you will find your mummy and daddy.' A hand came out of this portal and picked the girl up, and she was passed through it. Curious as to what was on the other side of this temporal hatch, Ian went upwards and poked his head through. He saw totally white grass all around him and everything else was brilliant, blinding white light. As he could see nothing more he came back down inside the ship, only to look down and see the body of the young girl floating dead in the water, her teddy nearby.

He later learned that the ship he found himself on was the *Herald of Free Enterprise*, a ferry that had overturned as it was coming out of the Belgian port of Zeebrugge on the night of 6 March 1987. The ferry was 'roll-on, roll-off', which meant cars and lorries could drive on and off the boat, through large doors that opened at the bow end. On that fateful night the boat went to sea with its bow doors still open and the sea flooded into the car deck, causing the ship to capsize just outside the harbour. In total 193 passengers and crew lost their earthly lives in the shocking disaster. I believe Ian was one of many helpers, called upon

The overturned Herald of Free Enterprise. *After such a disaster, the spirit world needed the help of the living to help so many souls cross over.*

perhaps by the spiritual world, to help the distressed dying cross over to their next life.

It seems plausible that a such a terrifying and sudden death could cause the confused spirit to remain in the earthly realm, and the box-like structure of the ferry may also have stopped it from passing on into the other side. Sometimes the discarnate personality may need an intervention from either a living or spirit helper to get to their next level of reality – rather like a consultant doctor might intervene to ensure a safe birth by performing a Caesarean section. And sometimes the spirits themselves may even reach through directly to our world to try and save the living.

A GRANDMOTHER'S WARNING

We don't fully understand the spirit world and although those in touch with it, like mediums, have a greater knowledge about this next phase of existence, when most people think of a ghost or spirit, they tend to think of something spooky and scary that is somehow out to get them. The events in the next story may well alter that perception.

In 1990 Dee was married to a British soldier stationed in Germany and was living there in army accommodation. At that time most of the British troops stationed there were actually in Kuwait fighting in the first Gulf War, which had started in August of that year. This included Dee's husband, an army engineer, so Dee was doing her best to bring up her two small children on her own most of the time. Her young son often kept himself amused by playing with a small toy car that was powered by batteries and had a wire attached to a controller that allowed him to steer it. At this point in time, though, it was broken and had no batteries in it. Despite this, one day Dee saw the toy car suddenly power up by itself and whizz across the floor, leaving her totally baffled.

A few weeks later, she went down into the cellar to get something from the freezer there and noticed the cellar light was turning on and off by itself. She could not understand how the light would do this and when she asked housing maintenance to check it out they reported that it was all in good working order, but couldn't provide an explanation for it turning on and off.

More time passed until one night Dee felt a strong urge to wake up and did so to a startling sight. She saw standing at the end of her bed two female human figures with sparkles of light all around their bodies. Dee said although she could see some parts of them very clearly, other parts appeared to have cracks, with gaps in their composition, as if she was looking at a reflection in a broken mirror. She recognized the figures as her grandmother and Mrs Brown, a former customer from when Dee used to work as a hairdresser. However, the two spectres had not actually known each other when they were both alive. Dee described them as wearing milkmaid-type bonnets on their heads. (Incidentally, it has been reported that similar attire has been seen on fully materialized spirits in seances.) This may have been a partial manifestation, with the bonnets there to fill in the blanks and help Dee to see the figures.

As both figures shimmered in a beautiful light, Dee's grandmother spoke telepathically to Dee, using her mind rather than speaking out loud. She said, 'You must leave! You must go, as one door closes, another one opens. But you must leave!' This was 'spoken' in a very strong, stern voice and then the images of the spirits began to dissipate. Dee quickly clambered to the end of the bed and reached out her hand to touch the fading apparitions as her grandmother and Mrs Brown dissolved into nothing. Their images faded, along with the magical sparkling light effect, until they were no more. Dee began to cry and begged them to stay but all she could see was the dark and silent room.

A SHOCKING DISCOVERY

When Dee's husband eventually returned from the Gulf War, something had changed in him and they began to have problems in their relationship. Dee had an overwhelming urge not to stay in the family home with him upon his return so she arranged for herself and her young children to move in with a friend who lived nearby. One day she decided to take her daughter to visit her husband, but he wasn't there. Having called out to him without receiving an answer, Dee told her daughter that she would get her an ice cream from the freezer in the cellar. When she went downstairs into the cellar she came across the terrible sight of her husband hanging dead by his neck, clearly deceased. Dee ran back upstairs and fetched help straight away but the shock of seeing her husband affected her so strongly she passed out and next woke up on a neighbour's sofa.

Dee and her children were still staying with a friend who had a spare bedroom. A few nights after her husband's death she was lying in bed between her two sleeping children, when she noticed a movement to her left. She watched incredulously as her deceased husband appeared, rising up into a sitting position next to her. He turned his head and looked at her and she noticed that his top lip was raised upwards and his face was slightly contorted. A shocked Dee shouted, 'Go away, go away!' while waving her hands over the materialized spectre, and the spirit of her husband promptly vanished. The atmosphere of the room returned to normal and Dee was able to fall asleep. Later, during her husband's funeral service, Dee looked into his open coffin and was very surprised to see his face was distorted, with his top lip curled upwards just like his spirit's appearance. She found out later that this was the result of the rope pulling up around his neck and causing the muscles to contort his face and mouth.

SPIRIT PROTECTORS

Things had begun to settle down a little for Dee when a member of the British army's military police came to update her on their investigation into her husband's suicide. The police officer revealed that her husband had manufactured two extra ropes and it was their belief he intended to hang the couple's two young children along with himself. Dee now came to understand that the manifesting spectres of her grandmother and Mrs Brown were trying to warn her to get away from the family home. They somehow knew that her husband was going to do something dreadful to his family and they had come to try and protect them from the actions of this sadly disturbed soul. Dee said she also learned that some spirits assist others with their energy to help them manifest or make a connection. Mrs Brown's spirit energy may have been serving to 'boost the signal', helping the grandmother's spirit get this critical message to her.

Looking back, Dee said she realized that the initial contact didn't happen when she saw the manifestation of the two spirits. She remembered the time when her son's toy car was driving by itself and the light was going on and off in the cellar, where her husband's death would later take place. For Dee, these were the first signs that the spirits of her grandmother and Mrs Brown were watching over her and decided they could not stand by and let tragedy unfold. Thankfully for herself and her children, she took their advice.

CHAPTER THREE

HAUNTINGS, STRANGE MESSAGES AND TIME SLIPS

When most people are asked about paranormal experiences, their thoughts jump straight to ghosts and hauntings. This is quite natural, because many of us have lost one or more people we love, and we've all grown up reading and watching ghost stories that both scare and excite us. The paranormal stories in this chapter will explore lingering hauntings by what many people perceive as ghosts – although in fact they may not be. This is because the term 'ghost', as we will see, is not as clear cut as you might assume.

As well as exploring 'typical' hauntings, and considering some alternative paranormal explanations, we will see that some experiences that appear ghostly could in fact be examples of a real-life 'time slip': that is, suddenly seeing the location they are in as if they were in exactly the same spot hundreds, and even thousands, of years ago.

WHAT IS A GHOST?

Sadly, many people suffer an unnatural, sudden death, sometimes involving great fear, pain and violence: for instance, if they are murdered or involved in an accident. Such an event can sometimes shock a soul into a state where they cannot move on and they become stuck between worlds or planes of existence. Whereas usually a spirit is free to go where it wishes and is a loving entity, a disturbed spirit may still be burdened by the emotions and physical issues it had in our reality, so it can be a very disturbing presence. What may also happen is that even if a spirit does move on to another world, their life force leaves a longstanding impression at a location where they died – almost like a recording of the event. The memory of that event can become what we also think of as a haunting. There might be many reasons why this happens, but there seem to be some common themes in many of these sightings. Shock, emotional trauma, painful deaths – all will leave a burden upon the person who dies to some extent.

Spirit entities eventually find their way to a higher spiritual plane through the help of those on the other side – that is, a more evolved soul acting as a spirit guide. They can also be helped through 'rescue mediumship', where a medium on this side of life tunes into the soul of the stranded individual, communicates with them and points them in the right direction. Often, this involves helping them comprehend that there is an afterlife and they have a soul. The 20th-century British medium Leslie Flint said many spirits actually came through his 'direct voice' mediumship asking why this spirit world was never explained to them during their physical life!

THE PSEUDO IMAGE

The late American author, poet and medium Jane Roberts channelled the spiritual entity or guide known as Seth, who had much to say on the topic of souls stuck in our plane of reality in a series of books known now as the *Seth Material*. Seth explained that the focus of the personality or soul is not as strong as it was in physical life, so it is not able to organize its own energy in those terms. A trapped soul tries to operate as if it were still in its earthly condition and habitually tries to construct a physical form of itself. This 'pseudo image' or form can be perceived and contacted by those who are psychically aware, such as mediums.

Souls who are trapped here as ghosts or spirits are focusing their attention at this level of reality because it was the only one they knew. Acting unconsciously, they try to carry on living as their earthly selves in this realm, but they are slightly out of tune with our reality and don't have enough energy to create a full form here. But they keep trying, again and again.

An example of this is the spirit of the young female patient who was found on the stairs of the hospital (see Chapter 2). She passed out of her earthly body and the new spirit body she now had was basically the same as the old, as her unconscious mind created it, as it does our earthly physical body. She managed to sustain the projection of her body for a short while before she was no longer perceived. Either a spirit helper from the other side came to assist her, or her focus in this reality changed, so that she phased out of perception in our world – rather like a radio going out of tune and losing the station that was broadcasting. In Jane Roberts' book, *Seth Speaks*, the spirit guide explains that those souls who do not realize that they are dead will be informed of their new situations. Spirit guides or helpers appear to help them understand what has happened to them.

WHO IS SETH?

Jane Roberts and her husband Robert Butts began experimenting with a Ouija board, among other methods, in 1963 for a planned book on how to use ESP (extra-sensory perception). They initially received some communications through the board from a spirit claiming to be Frank Withers – the name of a man who had lived in their local area, Elmira in New York State. 'Frank' continued to communicate with Jane and Robert, but after a few sessions Jane began to somehow know the answers in her mind before they were expressed by the glass moving on the board.

The spirit then said he would use a higher self, or more evolved part of Frank's consciousness, to continue communicating with Jane. Rather than communicate through the board, Frank's higher-self personality would now come through Jane while she was in a trance and use her vocal chords to speak through her. He went on to say that he could now be called 'Seth'. In further trance sessions Seth talked about human existence, the nature of reality, and existence in this world and the next, including reincarnation and other complex concepts of consciousness.

Jane channelled the Seth entity for nearly 20 years and he was said to have written many books through her, until her death in 1984. The *Seth Material* is a compelling resource for anyone researching the afterlife and related subjects. Seth spoke in particular about communication between the living and souls who have recently passed on. But what about the countless cases from around of the world where people have seen apparitions that do not appear to be the recently dead, but instead seem to be playing out their actions as if they were still alive in this reality? Are these a stranded soul, or more a kind of living memory, or even a recording, of the past?

STONE TAPE THEORY

As already discussed, ghosts are very different from spirits. Ghosts appear in the same location over a long period of time, so much so that stories circulate about their sightings, often becoming local legends. Some researchers think ghosts are more 'thought forms', created unconsciously by the people who were present at a traumatic or emotional event that happened long ago in that location The emotional energy generated by the event was so strong, it causes a 'recording' of these feelings to be made. Rather than a soul stuck between worlds, this is more like an old film replaying itself.

One version of this, called the 'stone tape theory', suggests that ghosts are recordings made on to the stones of the buildings where they are seen. Supposedly the stone itself acts like the magnetic tape in an old-fashioned tape recorder, imprinting memories and emotions around that event and then replaying them for others to see later. For example, it's possible that the stones and soil of old battlefields have effectively recorded those violent, chaotic and distressing events. The many thought forms sent out by the participants of that time might be witnessed later on by those sensitive enough to see them. So soldiers might be seen running past, or the sounds of the battle might be heard on occasion. The site at the battle of Culloden, near Inverness, Scotland, between the English and the Scots which occurred in 1746, has many reports of a tall man with drawn features and dressed in tartan clothes walking around the area. When approached he is heard mumbling the word 'defeated'. After the American Civil War battle of Gettysburg in 1863, people have claimed to have seen ghost soldiers in the area, and sometimes even ghost battles occurring.

Of course, not all ghost sightings take place around the locations of battles from the past, driven by chaos and fear. Their presence could reflect the more mundane activities of daily life, or the inevitable death of literally everybody and the sadness that generates for those who are still living here.

VICTORIAN MOURNERS IN THE BACK GARDEN

Paranormal researcher Christian Delaney experienced a very interesting ghost episode in 1980 when he was around eight years old and living in a house in Shropshire, UK, that had been used by the local undertaker (funeral director) many years before. He woke up one night and saw what looked like a coffin lying there in the room with a blue light surrounding it. Frightened, he stuck his head under the blankets until he was able to get back to sleep.

On a different night, he happened to be looking out through his bedroom window at the full moon casting its light across his back garden on to his swing. As the clouds partially cleared to reveal more light, he noticed what appeared to be a tall, thin man wearing a top hat and swishing a long stick as he slowly walked across the garden near the swing. It was so bright Christian could even see the man had sideburns, which made him think the mysterious figure might be from the Victorian era. Following this man were groups of other people either holding up the coffin or following it in a procession across the garden, all in similar Victorian dress. As the clouds moved across the night sky and obscured the moon, the image seemed to fade out. But when the moonlight returned the image became stronger again.

Christian's observation about the moonlight is interesting as it suggests a certain wavelength of light may have helped this scene to manifest. In controlled seances, natural daylight actually seems to impede the physical materialization of spirits. Perhaps, then, we associate hauntings with night time because the conditions are more suitable for this type of apparition. After all, the full moon often features in ghost stories!

These were probably not stranded spirits but more likely in my view a recording made on the atmosphere. A funeral is both a highly emotional outlet for grief and a ritual that makes the bereaved face the reality that a loved one is gone, so the ghosts could have been generated partly by the repeating raw emotion of the many funerals that were linked to this site, as the location of the funeral director. Christian, who felt he had some sensitivity, was able to perceive the scene aided by the moonlight. It is also interesting to note that in typical ghost stories, the full moon is often featured as part of the setting. Does Christian's strange tale mean that ghosts are more likely to be spotted at any location associated with funerals, just as ghost hunters often head for cemeteries? If you believe some of the paranormal tales later in this chapter, perhaps not.

SURVIVAL PERSONALITIES

Some areas seem to be more receptive to recording or holding on to these 'thought-form' apparitions and it takes a range of conditions to be able to access them. Some have suggested that an electromagnetic effect is possibly involved. The type of person picking up the thought form may be psychic in general, or good hypnotic subjects. Or the person witnessing such phenomena may shape it to their own cultural background such as religious icons. Visions of the Virgin Mary are common in Catholic countries, for example. Not all will be fulfilled and, if they are, maybe only partially or for a limited time. Seth the spirit guide explained that some apparitions are thought forms created by the living, rather than the dead, and these 'survival personalities' arise out of a person's long-held anxieties. They behave in the same way as the living person and are in themselves quite harmless. According to Seth, living people can also appear on occasion as ghosts in other levels of reality! Let's return for a moment to my brother's paranormal experience, when he saw an apparition of our mother before she even died. In this case, I believe her thought form or inner self was not sent out due to a lingering deep anxiety, but more because she was sensing freedom to come, when she would eventually leave her physical body behind. In my view people are rather like television stations broadcasting thought-forms without knowing it and occupants of other realities may see these as ghostly figures, like a TV audience sees images on screen.

There are also accounts of people who have encountered ghosts or perhaps thought forms from other time frames – and the apparitions seem just as startled to see the living who have spotted them. Author Irene Allen Block saw a form of a maid in her son's house, in London in 2004, who was just as startled to see her. Her son, Jamie, used to see her often standing at the top of the big staircase when he used to come home from a night out. She would just stand there watching him as he came through the door. This suggests our world can sometimes bleed through to the past and vice versa. Jane Roberts said in her writings (or Seth's, depending on your point of view) that no systems are closed. She meant that our world is open to other worlds beyond our perception just as those worlds beyond are also open to others beyond them. The *Seth Speaks* book describes 'co-ordination points', which are places in our world where energy flows more quickly and freely between one reality and another. This could potentially help to explain portals, those entry and exit points between dimensions that featured in some of the strange experiences already related here, like the Native American spirit guide emerging nightly from a bedroom cupboard seen in Chapter 1.

THE PRESENT SEES THE PAST

Roger Kent, a leisure centre worker, had an experience of the present somehow 'seeing' the past. He owned a house in one of the Orkney islands off mainland Scotland, which he thought must have been one of the island's oldest inhabited residences, and possibly connected to a monastery. Roger reported often looking at the flagstone-floored hallway and seeing the clear figure of a monk sitting on a stool who was lit by the fire from a stone or brick fireplace that was no longer there. Roger said he could even see the firelight flickering on the monk's face as he kept warm and chatted to another, unseen, person. Did the monk's emotions and thoughts in his own time create this later apparition? Maybe either the monk or the unseen person he was talking to was in emotional turmoil. Whatever the truth of this situation, it is fascinating to think that Roger could have been experiencing stone tape theory in action.

Another feature of this ghostly encounter was the lack of sound; Roger could see the monk was talking to the other invisible person, but could not hear his voice. It's often said that the sound associated with ghosts and hauntings often seems to disappear after they have been sighted for around 200 years. It's as if these ghostly replays have a shelf life, with the audio being the first element to deteriorate. That could also explain why dinosaurs don't seem to haunt this world. However, this absence of sound does not appear to always be the case in hauntings, as illustrated in the next strange tale of one of the most famous ghostly sightings anywhere in Britain.

ROMAN LEGIONARIES MARCH IN YORK

During the cold February of 1953 in the northern English city of York, a young apprentice plumber named Harry Martindale, who was aged 18 at the time, was part of a team of plumbers and heating installers working on behalf of the National Trust at the Treasurer's House, a historically significant Grade 1 listed building. The workers were situated all over the building and young Harry was set to task in the basement area, where he was up a small ladder helping with the installation of pipes. He had placed his ladder in a narrow trench in the floor to help secure it better. Unbeknown to him, this trench had already been partially excavated by archaeologists, revealing a section of a Roman road that had run partly through the grounds before the house was even built.

Harry had been working for about four hours by himself when he heard strange noises nearby. He thought it sounded like music but it seemed to consist of only one note, like a horn or trumpet being continually blown. He assumed it was possibly a wireless radio somewhere nearby on another floor, and he continued to work. The noise started getting much louder and sounded like it was coming through the wall near to where Harry was working. Eventually it got so loud that he looked down from his ladder to see a Roman soldier walk straight out of the wall! He described the soldier as wearing a helmet with a plume of feathers and a metal strap that tied at the chin and a full military uniform. Even stranger, Harry could only see the Roman

The spirits of Roman soldiers could be seen walking through York.

from the knees up as he marched forward, but as he approached the trench that had been excavated, the lower legs of the soldier revealed themselves in full, including his feet in open sandals.

Amazed at what he was seeing, Harry leant back too far on his ladder and promptly fell off it. He picked himself up and quickly scrabbled into the corner of the cellar to try and avoid detection. However, the Roman soldier did not even glance over in Harry's direction, despite the noise and movement Harry made by falling off the ladder. The soldier continued marching straight through the cellar and out through the other wall. Just as Harry thought he could make a dash for the exit, he heard more sounds, but this time it was a clanking, hoof-like noise.

GHOST WAR HORSE

Harry then saw a huge horse coming through the wall, with a proud-looking Roman soldier mounted on it, carrying a round shield on his left arm. As with the first soldier, the horse's lower legs could not be seen until it walked through the trench of the Roman road. Harry noticed the hooves of the horse were unusual, with quite bushy hair around them like a cart horse. Once more the rider completely ignored Harry as he trotted the horse through the cellar and vanished through the end wall. It was not over yet: Harry now heard more footsteps and this time even more Roman soldiers marched through the wall in rows of two.

Harry was too nervous to even think about counting them, but he later estimated there to be about 20 soldiers. Particularly interesting was the sound: Harry's strange experience was heralded by the sound of the horn and he could also hear the men chatting among themselves, although in a language he could not understand. (Roman soldiers when returning from a battle would usually announce their arrival by blowing a large horn so their garrison knew they were coming.)

Harry went on to describe the soldiers as rather unkempt and not clean shaven, and some as having mud on their tunics. He said they were not transparent or semi-solid but looked like totally solid beings – in fact, he said that had he been brave enough, he would be able to reach out and touch one! He described them as tired, worn out and scruffy. Notably, they carried round shields and wore their swords on their right side, not the left that was more typical of Roman legionaries. Also, their tunics were green rather than the red most people would associate with Roman soldiers. Harry noticed one soldier walking to the side of the others who was carrying a long tube-like contraption that he later thought might have been the source of the horn sound he heard.

FORGOTTEN IMPERIAL ARMY

Historians questioned Harry some years after his experience, and from his description of the ghosts pieced together that these particular soldiers were probably from the later Roman Empire. They had doubts about Harry's descriptions of the green tunics, round shields and small swords worn on their right side. But York was home to one of the main Roman forts in Britain at the time and it's likely these soldiers were left behind by the empire to defend its outer reaches in Britain, and thus were a forgotten imperial army.

They were described by archaeologists as 'auxiliary' soldiers, or back-up troops possibly recruited from the local populace. Soldiers like this would have been walking down the Roman road back to their base after being away for maybe a few days defending the east coast of northern Britain. Key to pinpointing them as auxiliaries was the round shields, which native-born Roman soldiers were unlikely to have carried. Only experts on the imperial Roman military would be able to identify this feature, along with the green tunics of auxiliary troops, so this was a really compelling part of Harry's account.

Understandably, poor Harry was frightened out of his wits and as soon as the last of the soldiers marched past him he made his escape and ran up the stairs of the cellar where he came face to face with the elderly warden of the building. The warden looked at him and said, 'By the looks of you my lad, it looks like you've seen them Roman soldiers!' Apparently, about a year earlier the warden himself had seen exactly the same ghosts down in the cellar but decided not to tell anyone for fear of ridicule. Harry immediately took sick leave and never returned to his job as a plumber's apprentice. He would not go anywhere near the cellar for another 25 years, when a TV film crew made a short documentary on his experiences there and he was persuaded to go back down and take part.

MORE ROMAN SIGHTINGS

Harry and the warden were not the only ones who claimed to witness the Romans in the basement of the Treasurer's House. A few years later, in 1957, the new warden was a woman by the name of Joan Olson, who owned two terrier dogs. One morning, she was doing her daily tasks and let the dogs run ahead of her and they managed to get access to the cellar where a few years earlier Harry had experienced his ghostly encounters. She heard her dogs howling and snarling at something in the cellar and went down to investigate. She peered through the door to the cellar and looked down to see what her dogs were snarling at and she saw, just like Harry did, around 20 Roman soldiers marching through the very same wall.

She described them as splattered in mud and looking worn and tired. It was almost an exact repeat of the scene that Harry had observed a few years earlier. They marched right through the basement and again vanished through the end wall of the cellar. A few months later, Joan was near the same place and heard marching again. She looked into the cellar to see the same soldiers as before, but this time each soldier was leading a horse of his own along the old Roman road that ran through that part of the house.

PAST AND PRESENT ROMANS?

A few months later, in December 1957, Joan once again saw the Romans with their horses passing through the cellar. On this occasion the soldiers were slumped over on their horses, almost as if they were worn out or sleeping as the horses were trotting them back to their fort. These soldiers looked the same as before, with the same uniforms, and both the horses and soldiers were again splattered with mud. Now this is an interesting point to note, although whether it has merit to the story or not, I do not know. In all the descriptions the soldiers and the horses appeared to be splattered with mud. This suggests that the 'recordings' of these ghostly scenes are likely to have happened in the autumn or winter months, when there tends to be more rain, causing the ground to be muddy.

Studies show that the weather in Britain around that time was not as wet as you might think, as scientists studying tree-ring growth have found at that time that it was sufficiently warm in northern Britain for grapes to be grown there. It also suggests that the ghostly soldiers had gone off the Roman road and into muddy fields. Both Harry and Joan's respective sightings were in the winter months. So rather than a ghostly recording of the soldiers being played back, as in the stone tape theory, the witnesses could have been seeing back into a past that was still playing out simultaneously with their present time.

For example, let's say Joan's timeframe, December 1957, is somehow synchronized with the Roman timeframe 2,000 years earlier, around December 100 BCE. If someone happened to be in the cellar and saw activity during the summer, they might possibly see marching Roman soldiers with no mud on them, because in the Roman period it is also their own summertime. This could explain the differences in the sightings of the soldiers, whose actions varied each time. If this was a ghost recording, witnesses would have seen exactly the same scene and actions over and over again. However, it seems they saw the same characters but in different 'episodes' of their lives. It's as if two cogs of time were synchronized and turning simultaneously, but with one further back in history.

A WINDOW THROUGH TIME?

It has been stated that time exists all at once, but in our world we perceive it moment by moment. Think of this like an old analogue television that only lets you watch one channel at a time, and sometimes suffers with occasional 'ghosting', or cross-channel interference from other stations, depending on the weather. One second, you may be watching your regular daytime soap opera, and the next, perhaps due to atmospheric conditions, Charles Dickens' *A Christmas Carol* is suddenly playing on your screen showing scenes from Victorian London. The Roman ghosts could be like that, and in certain conditions, some people are able to catch a glimpse of them.

Harry stated the Romans took no notice of him, as they could not see him. For them, Harry was not there: all they could see was their landscape and the road back to their Roman fort, which would have lain below the level of the present house. Without the trench dug by archaeologists in the cellar, the Romans would likely not have been seen at all. Digging down could have created a window into the past, which suggests there could be many ghosts walking under our feet quite unknown to us. Perhaps, being almost enclosed, the cellar helped to contain the energy needed in order to manifest the soldiers and their horses, as described in earlier chapters. But I feel Harry's story and the repeated sightings represent more of a peek through a window to different points of time in the same Roman era, rather than a stone tape theory-style energy 'recording'. They appear not to be ghosts in the typical sense – that is, trapped souls that are re-enacting a traumatic event, such as battle or violent death. Instead they may simply be participants in history, observed through an open portal through time. The next paranormal story takes this concept even further, as many believe it is evidence of direct communication through time, but in this case by means of a rather old-school computer!

THE DODLESTON MESSAGES

In the 1980s Ken Webster was a newly qualified teacher at Hawarden High School in the Welsh border region. He was loaned a new (at the time) school computer so that he could practise using it at home, an old cottage in the English village of Dodleston in Cheshire. Ken lived there with his girlfriend Debbie and their friend Nic, who lived in the attic room above them. The computer, a BBC Micro, was a basic word processor with no internet connection (still a developing technology in those days) that was plugged into the wall for power. It could not receive signals, emails or web pages, and simply let the user create and organize text documents via typed commands on the keyboard.

One night the household were enjoying Christmas drinks at a friend's house, having accidentally left Ken's computer in the menu mode, or standby mode as we would say today. When they returned, Ken noticed an extra file had been created on the drive, called 'KDN' or 'Ken, Debbie, Nic' if you like. The file seemed to be a rather abstract message addressed to the household, talking about flowers seeking the light, bodies no longer in pain, and pussy cats seeking fortune in London.

Ken thought that the message was a joke put there by a friend of his, who often popped around to record guitar tracks with him. Still, the message unnerved him somewhat. He returned the computer to the school and borrowed another the following year, 1985. Again, at one point it was left on accidentally, and a new message appeared. This one was more complex and direct and the author claimed it was written on behalf of many others, apparently in an early modern English style. This message described observations made about Ken and his girlfriend Debbie and the décor of the house. It suggested that the house had once belonged to the messenger and was signed with the initials 'L.W.'.

Ken's fellow teacher, Peter Trinder, examined the messages and concluded they were from either the 16th or 17th century. Between them, Ken, Peter and another friend who was a solicitor, composed a reply to the mysterious 'L.W.' who had apparently taken control of the computer. They asked about the time that L.W. was inhabiting, which they thought to be about 1620, and whether he wanted to know more about their present time, indicating that they lived in the reign of Queen Elizabeth II.

A REPLY FROM 1521

The trio then went to the local pub for a few drinks. When they returned there was a reply from L.W. on the computer! He described his time as March 1521, during the reign of King Henry VIII. More correspondence followed between the two parties, with 450 years' time difference between them! 'L.W.' eventually gave his full name as 'Lukas Wainman'. He claimed he had lived in Ken's house and seemed to think that Ken had stolen it from him and was using strange lights fashioned by the Devil, referring to electric lights. He also mentioned his visits to another village to see a friend. It seemed odd, though, that he was aware there were lights in the house but also asked Ken 'if he hath a horse?'

Even more confusing was the modern English usage in some parts of the message: for instance, question marks and brackets, which were not in use during the reign of Henry VIII. Was this some kind of prank played on Ken by his friends? If so, how did the prankster manage to reply when no one was in the house at the time? Ken's friend Peter did further research and identified certain words used by 'Lukas' in early modernEnglish mixed with some Latin as a dialect that originated in Cheshire in the 16th century. He also matched the sentence construction with the same dialect. The messenger appeared to be very knowledgeable about the materials found around Ken's house, or more specifically under it, stating that the house was made with red stone, which was later found to be true.

When Ken wrote to 'Lukas' that they came from the year 1985 he seemed startled and replied that he thought Ken and his friends were all from the year 2109 like 'his friend' who had brought him 'the strange box of lights'. Was it possible that another correspondent from the future had somehow given 'Lukas' some kind of lightbox or computer from 2109 that could communicate across time?

CALLING 2109

Ken decided to try to send a message across time to 2109 by writing 'Calling 2109'. Later, another reply appeared on his computer. It addressed Ken, Peter and Debs and gave them a choice; '2109' could either explain everything to them, but this knowledge would affect their futures, or they could simply accept his assurance that all three of them had a purpose and during their lifetime they would change history. Then '2109' explained that they did not wish to affect Peter and the others' destinies by interfering too much, but could offer guidance instead. So it seems that Peter had opened two channels of communication, one past and one future. However, this story took a new turn when other communications occurred.

POLTERGEIST ACTIVITY

Ken and his housemates started to notice objects had been moved in the house. On one occasion Debbie arrived home to find all the living room furniture pushed up in a pile in a corner of the room, as if a giant had

In the 1980s, Ken Webster received email messages from a Tudor man who claimed to live in his house.

pushed it there haphazardly. Strange footsteps could be heard upstairs and Debbie began having dreams in which she met Lukas. They decided to ask the SPR (Society for Psychical Research) for help.

The SPR investigated but could not reach a definitive conclusion. Instead, they speculated that a tiny hidden microphone could have been used to record messages that the SPR had typed out to 'Lukas' and '2109' and then somehow sent the replies through the plug mains to the computer. But in 1985 the technology to do this was way beyond anyone's comprehension. Eventually they left, not even submitting a report back to the SPR, which was the society's standard procedure. Peter and the others were at a loss what to do next.

Then '2109' suggested they contact a UFO researcher called Gary Rowe, but after investigating he was not able to explain the messages – although he did believe they were actually coming from different time periods. Eventually, 'Lukas' revealed his real name was Tomas Harnden and that he used an alias to protect himself as he was living in a dangerous time (the 1500s). He said the 2109 being appeared to him in blazing green light inside his chimney and gave him the 'Leems Boyste', the name he gave the device he was using to communicate with Peter – which he activated by his voice, rather like an Alexa device today.

Spirits have been witnessed mysteriously floating out from chimneys – so maybe this isn't just a portal for travel used by characters in the *Harry Potter* stories. It seems a fairly common way of entering our reality from other places. Ken Webster went on to write about the time-travelling messages from the past and future in a book called *The Vertical Plane*, and a second edition with further material and expanded thoughts on his experiences was published 36 years later. Some claim to have debunked these mysterious messages, while others continue to believe they were truly paranormal in nature.

Debunkers point out that linguistic analysis on the BBC computer messages and those in Ken's book on the story shows the language to be extremely similar. Furthermore, Dr Richard Wiseman, a psychologist at the University of Hertfordshire, interviewed the two paranormal researchers from the SPR for the *Out of this World* TV programme which featured the Dodleston case and asked them what they thought it could be? They both said it was a complete hoax but declined to explain how it was done.

'CONVEXAUL MAGNETISM'

The '2109' being explained to Ken that the communications were possible because certain geographical areas have what it called 'convexaul magnetism'. Supposedly these cross-over points between magnetic lines running around the Earth cause distortions that can be picked up by sensitive individuals. This explanation sounds similar to the co-ordination points mentioned by the spirit guide Seth. So 'Lukas', or 'Tomas', in his time experienced this including his own poltergeist activity and so did Ken in his time, thus opening a line of communication between them. Maybe Ken, like Harry Martindale claiming to see Roman ghost soldiers in York, was actually interacting with a simultaneous moment in time, but in a different era. The explanation provided by 2109 is not really clear but does seem to border on the idea of ley line hunters who somehow tune into the lines of energy that they claim run throughout the land.

'I WANT CHOCOLATE!'

In 1993 Debra and Alex Sanders, a young married couple, were taking a break to a holiday cottage in a remote area of Dartmoor, a national park area in the south-west of England. The cottage sat at the end of a group of houses, and was very old. On their first night there, Alex could not sleep and hearing noises downstairs in the living room, he went to investigate. Debra decided to go downstairs with him to get a drink of water in the kitchen. When she walked in she got a shock: instead of finding it empty, she saw the figure of a young girl, around ten years old and dressed in vintage-style clothes, possibly Victorian. Debra nervously asked, 'Who are you?' and to her surprise the girl looked at her and said, 'I want chocolate!'

Debra noticed that rays of blue light were emanating from the back of the girl's head and streaming out in all directions. The girl turned away from Debra as if to leave the kitchen, and it was then that Debra noticed the source of the blue light – a massive injury to her head. The blue light was pouring out of it, and creating an aura effect around her. Debra suddenly got a mental impression of this girl either tripping and falling down into the cellar or being pushed, and this was the most likely cause of her death. The young girl said, 'I want chocolate!' again, then vanished. Astonished by this apparition, Debra ran back upstairs and waited in bed for Alex to return. A few minutes later he opened the bedroom door and put the latch back down on the door to secure it, saying, 'This house is as haunted as Hell!'

Alex explained that while he was in the living room investigating the noises he had heard, the living room lights were flickering on and off and he saw the faint impression of three soldiers who he thought resembled British army soldiers from the 19th century. He told Debra they were able to communicate with him using clairvoyance, another term for telepathic mind-to-mind communication. They told him they were the ones turning the lights on and off because they were absolutely fascinated with the electric lights and wanted to understand how they worked!

A cottage in Dartmoor proved to be a haunted house when a young couple holidayed there in the early 1990s.

He also received a mental impression of these soldiers out on the nearby moor with frost on their faces, dying from hypothermia. The British Army had trained soldiers on Dartmoor since the early 1800s, and some lost their lives there while on training exercises. An interesting adjunct to Debra and Alex's experience is that others staying in the house seem to have reported multiple hauntings by different characters from different eras. It seems that both the spirit soldiers and the young girl were unable to perceive each other in the house. Many mediums have said that some souls refuse to accept they have died and despite the best intentions of helpers on the other side, completely ignore offers of help, so convinced are they of the fact that in their mind, they have not died at all.

Debra and Alex decided their one night in their cottage would be their first and last and they would leave in the morning. After eating breakfast and packing their luggage, they were departing through the front door when Debra noticed a sepia-toned photograph of the house that looked like an image from many years earlier. The house, as it then appeared, looked like a grocery and sweet shop. Outside the shop stood the small figure of a girl and Debra was amazed to see it was the same girl who demanded chocolate from her in the kitchen the night before.

Looking at the photograph, it appeared the little girl must have lived in the house and might have been the daughter of the proprietors. She had sadly come to a tragic end, by either accident or intent. Maybe her true spirit had indeed gone on and this was the stone tape theory in action, recording her emotions in her death throes and her childish desire for chocolate all in one apparition. Of course it's hard to know, without further investigation into who the wandering frozen soldiers and the chocolate-loving little girl actually were.

Many people will struggle to accept purely anecdotal tales like Debra and Alex's experience. Unfortunately these usually occur without any warning or idea, so it's not possible to apply laboratory methods to investigate and either verify or disprove them. In my view, the recipients are probably sensitive to ghostly occurrences and another couple staying in the cottage would not experience the same kind of haunting. Harking back once more to Seth the spirit guide's coordination points, it does appear that south-west England may have more than its fair share, as the region seems to generate many anecdotal stories. The next encounter is another such paranormal occurrence.

THE WOMAN IN THE CHAIR

In 1967 Joan Brandine, a film repair technician, was around 19 years old when she went on a family holiday to a cottage in Devon. She had her own room and the window at the end of the bedroom looked out to a stunning view of the sea. One night she was sleeping peacefully when suddenly she spontaneously woke up in the middle of the night. Something made her glance to her left-hand side and there she saw a figure of an old woman sitting with her head facing down, slumped over as if asleep. Joan was very taken aback and although she thought the figure might have resembled her grandmother, she was too scared to look at it long enough to be sure. She turned her head away and hid under the blankets, finally managing to fall asleep. After a few hours Joan woke up again, as the first rays of sunlight were breaking out over the sea.

While taking in the spectacular dawn view, Joan remembered seeing the old woman who was slumped in the chair. Glancing back to the side of the bed, to her shock she saw the figure was still there! This time, the woman's head had fallen backwards instead of forward. Joan could not believe that this apparition was still there and may have been present for hours. As she looked at the figure, still not totally sure whether it was her grandmother, it slowly faded out of sight, possibly caused by the daylight flooding the bedroom. Most ghostly sightings seem to occur at night. While it's not an absolute rule, many mediums turn off electric lights and black out windows in their seance rooms because, as discussed later in this book, physical spirit materializations use a light-sensitive paranormal substance called ectoplasm.

There are some intriguing details in this experience. For instance, why did the figure manifest in a holiday cottage? And why did it appear to be asleep or dozing on and off? It's important to mention here that at this point of time, Joan's grandmother was still living. So it could be that Joan was not viewing a classic ghost of her grandmother, or a different person. She may actually have been witnessing the astral portion of the woman's consciousness, or her astral body as it is sometimes called. As noted in Chapter 1, many people believe that during sleep, the mind of the person can leave the body and travel around the world or even to other realities beyond this one. The late author Robert Monroe claimed to have discovered accidentally that he could leave his body and visit people, and learned later that he could go to other realities and afterlife dimensions.

It is interesting that in Joan's case, the ghostly figure vanished in the early hours of the morning. To believers, this points towards Joan's sighting happening at the same time as her grandmother was actually waking up in her own home. As her grandmother was slowly coming back to consciousness, her astral self might have returned to the physical body. I think the astral self sometimes leaves the body during physical sleep and wanders in a slumbering state while the mind is at rest – and we can be totally unaware this has happened. If it was Joan's grandmother in her bedroom, this wouldn't be a random choice of destination. She may have been thinking about her family who were away on holiday and missing them so much, her higher consciousness tried to reach them using astral travel. And remember that Joan said the figure appeared to be dozing in the chair. If her grandmother wasn't practised at astral travel, as is likely, maybe her astral body managed to reach the destination but the effort or her inexperience resulted in her 'falling asleep at the wheel'. The figure could have been only vaguely aware of what it was experiencing and most of it was likely to be a dream-like experience.

So astral travel could explain why Joan's 'ghostly' visitor appeared to be peacefully sleeping – which would be unusual in a haunting – and also why it did not fade away as a ghost might do, but remained close to Joan throughout the night. If this is what happened, Joan's grandmother was probably unaware that her astral self was also taking a break at the family's holiday cottage! The SPR has collected numerous reports of people sighting phantasms of the living rather than spirits or ghosts of the dead. Many people nowadays are able to leave their body more consciously than in the past, because today there is so much advice available on astral travelling and out-of-body experiences, whether in books, online or via in-person guidance. I suspect there is a lot more out-of-body and astral travel going on in the world than many people suppose. It does beg the question, though, could someone's higher self travel through time from the future?

TWO BRIANS AND A FUTURE TIME SLIP?

In 1991, a man by the name of Brian Smith, a gas fitter from Chesham, Buckinghamshire, in England, was enjoying a Spanish holiday with his wife; the couple had checked into a hotel room on the fifth floor. During the first night there, Brian said he was suddenly woken up for no apparent reason, but then saw a smartly dressed man in a suit walk through his hotel room and over to the balcony, then jump or fall over the side! There was no sound accompanying this scary scene but Brian recalled seeing everything in it in solid, three-dimensional clarity. Understandably it was a very upsetting and confusing experience for him. But as he already had an interest in psychical and paranormal events, Brian wondered if he might just have seen an event from the past repeating itself.

At the end of their holiday as the couple were checking out of the hotel, Brian decided to ask the receptionist if she had heard any previous reports of anything unusual happening in their room. She told him nothing out of the ordinary had ever occurred there, leaving Brian quite perplexed about what he was certain he had witnessed. However, about a month after returning to the UK, Brian received a phone call from the receptionist at the hotel in Spain.

The caller said they had been confused, and that she needed to clear something up with him. First, she made a point of checking Brian's full name, which he confirmed as Brian Smith. Apparently, another Brian Smith had booked into the same hotel room directly after Brian and his wife. The caller explained that she had to be sure the personal belongings the hotel was about to send to the second Brian Smith's family were going to the right address. She then explained that the other Brian Smith had dressed for the evening in his smart suit, gone to the balcony of the hotel room and, possibly losing his balance or misjudging the balcony height, fallen to his death. Brian was shocked to hear this news – even more so because he had somehow witnessed his poor namesake walking to his death, even though it hadn't actually happened yet!

While some people will say Brian simply had a dream – maybe because he might have worried about staying in a fifth-floor room – it is possible that he had some kind of precognitive projection. When he saw the stranger in his room the other Brian was still living, so it was no ghost or spirit apparition. Maybe, just as my brother had seen my mum skip through his bedroom a few weeks before her own passing, the other Brian Smith had sent a projection of his own consciousness to the hotel room where his death was going to take place. His consciousness could have been preparing itself for this event. However, this is only speculation, because we have no further information around this strange account.

Psychics and mediums often say that each of us has a higher self or 'super' version of our consciousness and it is this higher version of us that will often take the major decisions relating to our earthly life, unknown to the lower 'ordinary' self or personality. It may be that his interest in the paranormal world allowed 'our' Brian to psychically pick up on a rehearsal for the future by the other Brian's higher self. Or, as discussed earlier in this chapter, could it have been the recording of a highly traumatic future event, captured by the bricks and mortar of the hotel room and sent back to the past? That two Brian Smiths booked into the very same hotel room only a week or so apart is an even bigger mystery. While sceptics will argue it was mere coincidence, as the transfigured spirit of the Snow Queen said, 'There is more to this world than you know!'

CHAPTER FOUR
FAKE SEANCES AND TRUE MEDIUMSHIP

'Science is only just getting its grip on the door handle of this unknown paradigm,' noted the writer and medium Jane Roberts, writing about mediumship and the spirit world through the eyes of her spirit guide Seth. Actually turning that handle would involve significant investigation into this area of the unknown, and much of science tends to steer clear of anything paranormal. However, a few scientists and thinkers are willing to do so by rigorously observing and comparing the processes of those who claim psychic abilities, as we will explore later in this book.

Meanwhile, my personal experiences lead me to believe that there are many genuine mediums who are able to help us connect with the spirit world, but they suffer from the many deluded or deliberately fake mediums and seances that tarnish the reputation of genuine psychic phenomena. This chapter will illustrate both sides, describing examples of what I believe to be both false practice and true mediumship. The following chapter will go further, looking at some fascinating examples of the latter.

SPIRIT GUIDES

Traditionally, in physical seances, the spirit guide would act as a control and guardian to the proceedings. They would control the other visiting spirits by bringing them, usually one at a time, into the manifestation process. These spirits would likely never have done this before, and the spirit guide would help them. They would also introduce the evening to the Earth-based sitters or visitors and explain to them what was going on.

The spirits try and raise the energy levels for the evening's seance by encouraging laughter and singing. These are by nature positive and happy thoughts, and mental energy is created by those very thoughts. The spirits use those energies for their benefit to help either manifest or assist the medium doing clairvoyance.

There are indications that spirit guides can come and go with the medium they work with, in the same way you may work with different colleagues over your career. They tend to try and improve the spiritual development of the person they are assigned to work with, but this would also involve helping them develop the medium's skills as well. Some mediums will stay as mental- or clairvoyance-skilled communicators all their lives, but if they have the ability to enter a trance or produce ectoplasm, another higher spirit guide may be called upon to assist in the development of that particular field. In the case of medium Helen Duncan, during her development, another guide took over from the previous one, who was by all accounts holding her back.

MENTAL AND PHYSICAL MEDIUMSHIP

The word 'seance' comes from the French word for 'session', from the older French *seoir*, meaning 'to sit'. Lots of people are familiar with the basic idea of attending a demonstration of mediumship, in a public hall or church. The medium will usually use what is termed 'mental mediumship' or clairvoyance, whereby the afterlife communicator or spirit will send telepathic messages, usually in the form of images, to the mind of the medium, who has to try and decode what the images are trying to say. Often the medium interprets these images wrongly, and has to go back mentally to their spirit communicator to request further information. At a seance you may see the medium look off to the side as they change their focus, almost daydreaming in order to let the images drop into their mind. These images may be combined with feelings, thoughts, ideas and sometimes names. Often, the medium doesn't receive

An early 20th-century seance.

free-flowing information spoken in clear sentences from the spirit. The process is like being given a photograph album and having to describe what you're seeing to another person who is blindfolded, without fully understanding what all the photographs are showing you.

Much rarer than mental mediumship, physical mediumship involves a spirit actually appearing as a solid being in the seance room. As outlined earlier in this book, the being materializes using a substance called ectoplasm that emanates during the seance, mostly from the medium and sometimes from the sitters (attendees). One famous physical medium was Helen Duncan, whose controversial activities during World War II are explored later in this chapter.

In physical mediumship the medium typically sits behind a curtain draped across the corner of a seance room, or in a 'seance cabinet': a purpose-built box about the size of a small wardrobe. The medium is very often tied or secured to the chair they sit in. This procedure is in place to prevent fraud on the part of the medium, to stop them getting up and walking around in the seance dressed up or mimicking spirits. Once everyone is satisfied that the medium is secured in their seat the medium will then relax and go into a trance or deep sleep. By going into a sleep state, the mind of the medium is set aside so to speak, allowing the guides or spirits to enter the proceedings. The spirit guide may then take over the voice box of the medium and begin to speak and direct the proceedings further. If conditions are considered right by the spirit guide, the seance may develop further into a full materialization session, where spirits will be able to extract the material known as ectoplasm from the body of the medium and form this into the shape of their former earthly selves, though this is quite rare and can be dangerous.

This form of mediumship requires very controlled conditions, with the medium typically gagged and tied to a chair inside the cabinet, partly to rule out accusations of fraud. Usually the medium sits in the dark and goes into a trance, or altered state of consciousness. Outside in the seance room, the voices of one or more spirit guides are often heard.

Once the right seance conditions are met, spirits will begin to manifest behind the curtain or inside the cabinet. The deceased personality draws the misty, viscous substance called ectoplasm out of the medium and it may also be drawn from the sitters or audience members. This mysterious substance is then used by spirit to mould and form the shapes of various body parts and becomes more solid, often forming hands and sometimes faces. On rare occasions, a fully materialized and full-body ectoplasmic form of a deceased person may emerge from the cabinet into the seance room, walk around and even speak with sitters. Residents of the spirit world have few opportunities to connect with sitters in this way, because relatively speaking there are so few people in the world who are able to perform physical mediumship.

RISKY BUSINESS

Physical mediumship does seem to come with a price. Mediums using this method often become ill later in life as the energy used seems to affect their own bodies, as if in each seance the medium gives off something that they never get back afterwards. It's notable that physical mediumship often seems to affect the medium's blood sugar levels, which can lead to diabetes and other long-term health problems. Helen Duncan, for example, took to eating cakes after each session and it's not unusual to see lots of discarded sweet wrappers at physical mediumship demonstrations or training sessions.

This kind of mediumship also appears to carry some risk for the medium during the seance itself. This is because a spirit's ectoplasmic form, once materialized, is said to be sensitive to daylight. It's believed that exposure to the wavelength of visible light causes the ectoplasmic spirit forms to be rapidly absorbed back into the medium's body. This can be quite dangerous, and severe burns to the body of mediums have resulted from this sudden exposure.

Psychic News magazine recently wrote about physical medium Scott Milligan, who suffered a burn after a rope that was partly lit by light was thrown close to his body when ectoplasm was present in the room. The Arthur Findlay College (an educational facility for mediumship) has also recently issued an eight-point safety protocol governing demonstrations of physical mediumship to try and reduce the risk of any harm coming to the mediums demonstrating.

(For another perspective on this issue, Chapter 7 describes one experiment that deliberately caused light to strike a manifested spirit named Katie King.) To avoid the potentially harmful effects of visible light, infrared lamps are usually set up in the seance room. This allows people to make out materialized spirit figures in the dim red light, rather like a photographer's darkroom. This kind of seance is usually directed by spirits from the other side because they fully understand the specific conditions required.

There is obviously another potential harm arising from spirits' light sensitivity. Because this type of mediumship usually operates in the dark, with dim red light and blacked-out windows, it is very often open to fake mediums taking advantage of sitters who are eager to hear from their deceased loved ones.

VOICE MEDIUMSHIP AND CLAIRVOYANCE

Physical mediumship is not always in the form of a spirit coming out from behind a curtain, greeting the sitters and bestowing them with wisdom. A variation is 'trance mediumship', where the medium goes into a trance-like state and is then taken over by a spirit so that they speak with a different voice.

The spirit wishing to communicate is usually an experienced and more advanced being than the average person, and they know how to reach this part of the mind of the medium, in order to operate their vocal chords and all the other complex physiology needed for human speech. Many of those who have passed over into the spirit world will not yet have reached that point in their development to be able to do this, so instead they tend to come through mediums who use clairvoyance. Trance sessions and clairvoyance do not require the windows to be blacked out or infrared light to be used because the spirit is not manifesting through the medium of light-sensitive ectoplasm. We will explore trance mediumship further in Chapter 6.

For me, accounts of mediums using darkened rooms with infrared lamps and producing only a trance voice will always raise a red flag. Another possibility is that an individual has somehow convinced themselves they have psychic abilities and performs a kind of delusional mediumship. You must decide for yourself whether the next accounts are examples of either fake or, at best, deluded mediumship. I attended both demonstrations outlined below and got a good opportunity to witness things at close hand.

WHAT A WONDERFUL WORLD

In 2017 in a seaside town in the south-west of England people arrived to see a medium called Chris. Audience members were given their own allocated seats to sit on and before the session began Chris had already set up his trance cabinet with a screen in front which could be rolled up to show the medium if required. He also demanded that he should be tied into his seat, to prevent him from moving around in the seance room. The room was then sealed in, so no one could come and go and the windows were blocked out with black paper.

The room was almost in total darkness apart from the red light from an infrared lamp. The CD player began playing the song *What a Wonderful World* by Louis Armstrong, with everyone in the audience asked to sing along. This was necessary, it was claimed, to help raise the vibrations that spirit entities needed to send through messages or use the body of the medium. As the audience continued to sing this classic song, an extra voice joined in – a deep voice with an American accent coming from inside the seance cabinet. However, this voice didn't seem able to keep in time with the music and also sounded like a poor imitation of a real American accent. After the song finished the voice announced it was none other than the man who made the song famous – the late singer and trumpet player Louis Armstrong!

It's reasonable to think that if anyone was going to sing this song correctly it would be the artist himself. Louis, or the voice claiming to be Louis, asked for the track to be replayed so he could sing along to it again. Even so, 'Louis' still had trouble keeping the tempo with his original recording. After the song had finished a second time, Louis went on to explain it was indeed a wonderful world and gave out messages of hope to everyone, before announcing he had to go.

A MINER, EX-BEATLES AND 'CRISPIN QUENTIN'

There was a long silence and then another voice started to come through. This northern English accent sounded like the speaker was from Yorkshire. He proceeded to tell people in the audience how hard his life had been as a miner in the Yorkshire coal pits. This discourse lasted for about 15 minutes, much longer than Louis' singing appearance. However, the miner didn't reveal anything about his identity that could be verified. Chris himself was from the north of England (although of course regional accents vary widely) so he would probably have had little trouble sustaining a Yorkshire accent.

After the miner had departed, the red light was turned off and the song *My Sweet Lord* by George Harrison was played on the CD. Following this, a supposed spirit guide's voice announced that George Harrison and John Lennon would physically materialize in the cabinet, come out and walk around the room, touching people on their shoulders. This would, however, happen in total darkness so there seemed to be no logic to John and George appearing and proving their spiritual existence if nobody could actually see or hear them! No infrared light would even be switched on to partly illuminate this spectacle, so anyone could have touched audience members in the darkness. Chris did not even produce the trance voices of John Lennon or George Harrison to support this claim.

By now the evening had turned into a kind of *Stars in their Eyes* show, with celebrity spirits lining up to speak from behind the curtain. The next voice shouted out 'Hello boys, lovely to be here this evening with all you nice men out there!' From the darkness came embarrassed laughter and the voice continued, 'It's Crispin Quentin here!' The laughter suddenly stopped as at least some in the audience understood this was a huge mistake – the voice should have said Quentin Crisp, the English writer and actor who was famous for his novel *The Naked Civil Servant*. The trance voice was exaggerating 'Crispin Quentin's' mannerisms and doing what seemed like a very poor imitation of Crisp. Like Louis Armstrong, who could not sing in time with his own song, this spirit seemed to forget his own name. He soon vanished to make way for the next spirit arrival.

SIR WINSTON CHURCHILL RETURNS?

Next on the set list of dead luminaries was the former British prime minister Sir Winston Churchill, certainly one of the most recognizable figures in the history of the 20th century. For this finale the curtain in front of the seance cabinet was drawn back and the red light switched on, so the audience could see Chris speaking supposedly while in a trance. However, this voice sounded like an average impersonation of Churchill. The 'spirit' of the great statesman said nothing special and memorable and nor was anyone in the audience allowed to address any questions to Churchill or any of the other 'spirits' presenting themselves either.

After the Churchill voice departed, the medium slowly came out of his 'trance'. It was quite a performance: he was untied from his chair as he emphasized to the audience that anything they might see could not be down to his sleight of hand, as his own hands were tied. This was odd in itself because nothing happened during the evening that a sceptic could attribute to sleight of hand, like strange lights or floating 'seance trumpets', which are metal cones used by spirits to amplify their voices.

The medium appeared to channel the spirit of Winston Churchill, but few were convinced by the performance.

Afterwards there was none of the excited chatter that so often happens after a really compelling demonstration of mediumship. No one even looked at the medium after or wanted to talk to him, which is also unusual. At least one audience member was heard saying they thought it was all complete rubbish. The main issue with this experience was that no returning relatives or friends from the other side were presented to the audience as strong evidence of their survival in spirit. No one personally knew any of the spirits that showed themselves. There was no evidence given by the celebrity spirits, or even by the Yorkshire miner, that could be checked later on. It seemed to demonstrate nothing other than poor imitations and limited knowledge of seance proceedings. The experience was in stark contrast to, say, the medium Jane Roberts, who conducted numerous voice mediumship sessions over many years in rooms that were naturally lit and full of people, and even on television, without once requiring any special red lighting.

THE SPIRITS OF CHRISTMAS?

In 2011, a Christmas-themed physical seance in one of England's home counties, near to London, was the setting for the next account – this time supposedly a demonstration of physical mediumship. In the seance room a Christmas tree complete with wrapped presents around its base had been placed near the seance cabinet. Attendees could not just turn up on the day, but had to write a letter to the host of the seance explaining who they were and their previous experiences of mediumship demonstrations. When they arrived they were searched and asked to hand over anything that might interfere with the seance, like a phone, camera, recording device or anything else that could affect with the proceedings. They were also told to sit in pre-allotted chairs.

The medium, William, was brought into the room by his wife and a short introduction was given to the audience about what they might experience. As it was Christmas, the audience were told by William's wife that the spirit children might unwrap the presents by the tree and throw them out to the sitters. William sat in the cabinet and was secured to his chair with Velcro fasteners and the curtain to the cabinet was drawn down in full view of the audience. The room lights were switched off and darkness ensued.

As with the previous account involving Chris, music was played supposedly to raise the vibrations of the sitters, to help along the manifestations. All the while William was, we were led to believe, going into a trance-like state in preparation for the mediumship demonstration. Sitting in darkness the audience could hear paper being unwrapped, then small toys landed on their laps. As the music faded, the sound of drums being played came from near the front of the room where a child's toy drum had been placed. When the drumming stopped, a seance trumpet appeared: this luminescent cone floated across the room and seemed to wave about. Typically in this form of seance, voices would be heard coming through the trumpet or cone, but in this case none were heard.

Later on, a voice from behind the curtain of the seance cabinet announced his presence as Jonathan, the spirit guide running the seance. The voice sounded like that of Richard Harris, the Irish-born actor who played the wizard Dumbledore in the first two *Harry Potter* movies, with a distinct Irish accent. Then Jonathan retreated, allowing a girl spirit to manifest her voice. This voice said she was called Marie and it was later claimed by William's wife that she was a French-Jewish girl aged eight who was born during World War II. However, her voice lacked any French inflection and sounded more like something from a children's television show where adults play childlike characters, like the Tweenies. (This was reminiscent of an incident at another seance, where a paranormal researcher encountered a 'French' spirit voice and decided to engage with it using the French he remembered from school. As he began to use various basic French phrases, the spirit suddenly announced that it had to return to the spirit world!)

Going back to the Christmas-themed seance, next the spirit guide Jonathan returned and announced there was now enough energy in the darkened room to allow him to materialize his hand inside the seance cabinet using ectoplasm and show it to the audience. The seance cabinet was now illuminated by the red lamp and a cover had been draped over the front of it, including over a lower section that was already open. William the medium's wife was sitting at the front, leading this segment of the demonstration.

A man seated near the front of the group was invited to lift up the draped cover and as he approached the cabinet, a human-looking hand reached out from inside. The audience member took hold of the cover as if to lift it entirely off the cabinet, and was immediately chastised by William's wife. She instructed him just to hold the 'disembodied' hand, and he said later that it felt real to him and it shook his own hand. As the materialized hand started to withdraw back under the draped curtain and into the cabinet someone in the room loudly said it was dematerializing. But some audience members reported seeing it slide back and then lift up off the floor, as if attached to a body. This body may well have been William the medium, who was inside the cabinet supposedly strapped with fasteners to his chair.

Jonathan spoke once more, saying there was now enough energy for everyone in the audience to form a queue to shake his ectoplasmic hand. The hand and some of the forearm were examined in turn by each sitter. 'Notice,' said William's wife, 'that this hand does not have a wedding ring on.' It was also free of any jewellery or clothing. Apparently this felt very much like shaking a hand with human warmth and flesh – it was not wet, waxy or otherworldly in any way.

Once everyone had shaken hands with 'Jonathan', the red light was switched off and music was once again played in the complete darkness. Then the music faded away and suddenly the main lights were switched on – to reveal William the medium who it seemed had materialized out of the seance cabinet still tied to his chair and in trance, a few feet from where he began his demonstration. Some people were apparently amazed at seeing what they thought was human teleportation. The medium was slowly roused from his sleep, supposedly unaware of anything that had transpired throughout the evening!

'HE AIN'T HEAVY, HE'S MY BROTHER'

William the medium's wife later explained more about the mysterious spirit guide, Jonathan. In his physical life he was supposedly a market trader from the East End of London. Yet when he spoke, it was with an Irish brogue rather than an East End accent. The medium himself was Irish and his brother was also later identified as sitting at the front of the audience that evening. Could William's brother have been the phantom drummer, as well as the spirit children who threw presents at people in the audience? And why would the medium's brother need to be present in the audience? He was seated near the drums and the Christmas presents that were alleged to have been unwrapped and thrown out to the sitters by the spirit children. It seems quite feasible that the brother dragged the chair, with William tied to it, out of the cabinet. The chair had smooth aluminium runner-style legs that could easily have helped it slide across a carpeted floor, with any noises masked by the loud music.

Once again, this demonstration didn't bring through any spirits that were actually known to the sitters, so there was nothing for them to verify by asking questions and no identifiers that could be compared with actual records. Compare this to reports about seances involving British physical medium Helen Duncan, which were often thronging with the spirits of sitters' close relatives and loved ones, all wanting to interact with them.

Later research revealed striking similarities between the Christmas seance described here and others hosted by William and his wife at other venues. One detailed review by a witness showed that events had occurred in exactly the same order, with the same voices of Jonathan and Marie, as another seance held four years earlier. It was almost if the whole session was scripted and rehearsed, like a magic show. Except the audience member who tried to pull up the seance drapes and look more closely was clearly not in the script!

CAUGHT RED-HANDED

I began this chapter by thinking how a scientific approach could help to expose fakery and, by extension, help to show that some mediums have a truly paranormal talent. How could this be applied to the Christmas-themed event and in particular the 'spirit' hand? Remember that all the guests to the seance were checked for potential recording devices and cameras. Nor were they permitted to check any of the equipment or room itself beforehand. Even so, in theory it would still be possible for an investigator to test out the bona fides of the spirit hand by applying a small amount of slow-drying red oil paint to their finger before the demonstration began. They could cover up the paint, for example with a plaster, so that it would look perfectly innocent if they have to undergo a search at the door – which can happen with physical mediumship demonstrations. It would simply look like an everyday injury with a protective plaster over it.

This hypothetical investigator would need to make sure they were the last one in the queue of sitters waiting to shake the materialized hand of the spirit guide. If they were to shake the spirit hand, they could remove the plaster just beforehand and the red oil paint would be smeared over the supposed spirit hand. Oil paints can take a few days to dry and, if painted on thickly enough it would still be wet to the touch and more importantly, spreadable. If it was really a spirit hand, the paint would have no effect and the hand would in theory dematerialize with no danger to the medium. If, however, the hand was human and the seance a fake, the paint would be very difficult to remove.

It would be highly unlikely that person pretending to be the spirit guide would have a bottle of paint thinner handy in their seance cabinet!

PUNCHY EVIDENCE

At the other end of the spectrum of physical mediumship to a fake hand is an experience that one sitter recalled as the most impressive piece of evidence he had ever personally witnessed at a mediumship demonstration. At the same venue, a few years previously, the host Ron saw a fully materialized Native American spirit guide who appeared to be around 7 ft (2.1 m) tall standing in the middle of the room. The guide asked a man to come out of the audience and push him hard in the chest. The man did so, and the guide did not rock backwards. The guide then asked the man to hit him hard in the chest and again did not budge an inch. Next, he asked the perplexed sitter to punch him as hard as he could in the chest. The man was reluctant, but did as he was asked, and the guide did not flinch or even slightly wobble. Instead, the spirit just vanished into the ground in a mist! If true, this would be an extremely difficult illusion to fake using trap doors and smoke machines, unless everyone else in the audience was in on the act.

Until there is irrefutable scientific proof of something as dramatic as a huge Native American materializing in a room full of people (and probably not even that would suffice for some people) the 'real or not real' debate will continue around mediumship and the existence of the spirit world. Organized religion has long taken either a hostile or dismissive attitude, based primarily on certain verses of the Bible. But it's surprising to think governments would even care, let alone throw their weight behind proving it as absolutely false. However, during so-called 'interesting times' this is exactly what can happen, as the next story shows.

HELEN DUNCAN, WARTIME MEDIUM

The physical medium Helen Duncan was so controversial that her activities were considered a risk to national security. Helen, or

'Hellish Nell' as she was nicknamed, fell foul of the British political and security authorities as a result of practising as a medium during World War II. Born in 1897 in Scotland, her parents recognized Helen's psychic talents from a young age. Supposedly she was able to ask for answers to questions in her lessons, which were then written on her slate board by an unknown force. As she grew up, local people would often ask for Helen's help. On one occasion, a local man went missing during a freezing winter and she was able to help locate him before he froze to death using 'remote viewing', or extra-sensory perception of images, sounds, feelings and other sensations that are arising elsewhere.

FORETELLING DEATH

After marrying Henry Duncan, Helen suffered a spell of pneumonia and while she was hospitalized she saw a vision of a coffin with her mother-in-law's name and date of death on it. Nine months later, Henry's mother died on the very day that was shown in Helen's psychic vision. Later, Helen's father-in-law seemed to be recovering from a short illness, but Helen also saw that he would die very soon. A few evenings later Helen was woken up by Henry's familiar knocking on their front door, although she also heard strange wailing noises around their house. Later the same night, a family friend knocked on the door and informed them that Henry's father had just passed away.

Helen's physical mediumship skills developed to such an extent that she would eventually get letters every day from around the UK requesting sittings with her and invitations to hold seances. Helen charged a small fee for her demonstrations and became the family's main breadwinner as Henry was too ill to work (she often paid for medical treatment for local children as there was no National Health Service at this time). Helen was regularly giving demonstrations at the Scottish Spiritualist Society's headquarters in the 1940s. The society was so impressed, they recognized her abilities by awarding her a certificate for her contribution to mediumship.

Helen Duncan was a medium whose abilities brought her into conflict with the government during World War II.

CHANGING SPIRIT GUIDES

Helen's first spirit guide, in life a man named Matthew Douglas, was reported to be dangerously erratic during seances, and even threatened to kill her. (It's interesting to note the story of another psychic who reported that his wife, a medium herself, was suffering from an energy overload as a result of her spirit guide's activities while she was in a trance, which was thought to be a danger to her. It appears that the medium was able to send a request to the spirit world to remove the first spirit from duty and replace it with a more experienced guide.)

In 1927 another spirit called Albert Stewart stepped in and became Helen's permanent guide. Albert announced himself to sitters as being born in 1883 in Scotland, where he lived with his parents until later emigrating to Australia and becoming an apprentice pattern maker. He explained that he died in 1913 from drowning when he was only 33 years old. He was described by most who encountered him as a much more peaceful presence than Matthew, and Helen's mediumship improved greatly under his care. He became highly respected by Helen and members of her family, who often called him 'Uncle Albert'.

Unusually, Albert also made himself known outside the seance room. When Helen was undergoing a hysterectomy, a male voice was heard declaring that the surgeon had cut far enough into poor Helen. Of course it could have been a prank, but no one in the operating theatre admitted to being behind the mysterious voice, which reportedly sounded like an Australian accent. When informed about this later, Helen's husband Henry declared it was Albert stepping in to look after Helen. It was also said that Albert had tried to warn Helen of danger before a raid on a demonstration she was hosting at a psychic centre in Portsmouth, advising her not to admit anyone in a naval uniform and again a few days later, not to admit a group of three men. Unfortunately, as we will see, Helen did not heed her spirit guide's advice.

SINKING SHIPS

Many bereaved people turn to spiritualism during wartime, and World War II was no different; interest in communication with the afterlife soared in Britain as so many people were losing loved ones on active service and as a result of air raids on cities and sinking of merchant shipping. Some saw this as an opportunity to cash in on the misery of the bereaved and their desperation to see or talk to their loved ones again.

Helen's reputation, however, was growing, primarily because of her reported skill in physical mediumship – where spirits materialize in the seance room – and due to the accuracy of the information given to people who attended. As word spread, it began to attract the attention of military and naval chiefs.

By 1941, Helen was doing physical mediumship demonstrations and seances in Portsmouth, the main port of the Royal Navy. When British warships like HMS *Hood* and HMS *Barham* were sunk it would often take three months before the public back home was informed. Understandably, the British government and navy wanted to keep news about recent sinkings from getting out to avoid damaging morale at home and giving propaganda victories to the enemy, and also to stop the German air and naval forces discovering the real extent of their impact on the British naval fleet. Plans were being secretly formulated for the D-Day invasion that would see thousands of Allied troops landing along the northern coast of France to push into mainland Nazi-occupied Europe. This was to be the largest amphibious invasion in history, so the British military and naval authorities and security services were determined to ensure it remained a secret.

However, it seemed that dead men were telling tales about lost Royal Navy ships, according to reports of Helen's regular seances. At one Portsmouth demonstration in 1941, Helen's spirit guide announced to a shocked audience that one of His Majesty's ships had sunk with the loss of many lives. Suddenly a dead sailor calling himself Sid materialized behind the seance cabinet, stepped out before the seated audience and announced that he had died during the sinking of HMS *Barham* in the Mediterranean. He said that the *Barham* had been torpedoed and gone down with all hands. Sid further claimed he had been burned to death in the explosions. He spotted one of his relatives in the audience that evening and made himself known to them. The news of the sinking was considered top secret. Something had to be done to silence Helen and prevent highly sensitive information leaking out from paranormal 'loose lips'. Her guide Albert had previously, in another seance in late May 1941, spoken about the sinking of HMS *Hood*, saying 'a great British battleship has just been sunk'. Brigadier Roy C. Firebrace, a high-ranking British Army officer, was one of those present in the audience. He checked with naval authorities later who had no knowledge of the sinking. But later it was confirmed that indeed the *Hood* had been torpedoed by the German battleship *Bismarck*.

FRAUD OR SMEAR CAMPAIGN?

Spies from naval intelligence posing as ordinary members of the public were instructed to attend one of Helen's seance's in January 1944. When a physical materialization of a spirit emerged from the seance cabinet, they suddenly switched the lights on, shouted 'Fraud!' and called in the police. One witness later claimed they grabbed the spirit's ectoplasmic form as it spread out on to the floor and that the 'ectoplasm' was actually a piece of cheesecloth. But when the police arrived no such material could be found, and it was never produced at Helen's later trial. She was also said to have been hurt in the raid as a result of the main lights being switched back on without warning, as discussed earlier.

Helen was promptly arrested and charged under an archaic law, the Witchcraft Act of 1735. This forgotten law referred to conjuring up evil spirits, and harked back to a time when witchcraft was widely thought to be real. It formed the basis for prosecuting her, even though she had never claimed to be a witch. On the night her seance was raided, there had been no mention of evil spirits.

PSYCHIC MEDIUMSHIP ON TRIAL

The authorities were obviously reluctant to allow any discussion of lost ships like HMS *Barham* in open court. In fact, during Helen's subsequent trial at the Old Bailey in London in 1944, there was never any mention of dead sailors returning and talking about how they lost their lives during the sinking of ships like HMS *Hood* or *Barham*. If the prosecution had raised the subject of these spirits emerging from the seance cabinet, it would have necessarily led to a further examination of the evidence, which could have supported Helen's claim of being a genuine medium.

Instead, the prosecution focused on the seance in question where the audience members jumped up and switched on the lights. They leaned heavily on the evidence of one particularly interesting 'expert', the psychical researcher Harry Price, who believed all mediums to be fake unless they could prove otherwise. Price claimed that Helen must have hidden cheesecloth under her clothes and even suggested that she swallowed it and somehow regurgitated it into the shape of human figures using some kind of a second stomach! He based this argument on the fact that Helen refused to undergo an X-ray. Moulding such complex figures from cheesecloth would have been a difficult feat in itself, even if Helen had not been tied to a chair inside the cabinet in a darkened room.

The trial of Helen Duncan began at the Central Criminal Court, known as the Old Bailey, in central London on 23 March 1944. Given that the prosecution witnesses were secret naval spies who deliberately provoked the seance room raid, many spiritualists throughout Britain thought that Helen was being persecuted. At that time she was a very high-profile medium and frequently featured in newspapers of the day. Even Winston Churchill thought the prosecution was a farce and too great an expense in wartime, as the Old Bailey was usually reserved for murders and other major criminal cases. After the trial, Churchill wrote to his Home Secretary, Herbert Morrison, complaining about the misuse of court resources on the 'obsolete tomfoolery' of the charge. On 3 April 1944, he said 'Let me have a report on why the

Witchcraft Act, 1735, was used in a modern Court of Justice.' He wanted to know what the cost had been to the State, writing that court witnesses had been brought up from Portsmouth and put up for two weeks in a 'crowded London', and that the Court Recorder had been kept busy 'with all this obsolete tomfoolery, to the detriment of necessary work in the Courts'.

Nevertheless, Helen Duncan was found guilty of fraudulent 'spiritual' activity under section 4 of the Witchcraft Act and imprisoned for nine months. The D-Day landings went ahead as originally planned.

ECTOPLASM OR CHEESECLOTH?

Although the materialized spirits at Helen's seances could only be seen in dim red light, many reports confirm sitters recognizing dead relatives or friends materializing in the seance room through the use of ectoplasm. This mysterious supernatural material only manifests during seances and it has been variously described as viscous, milky fluid and mist-like. During her trial, many supporters of Helen came forward and gave their testimony in defence of her abilities. One witness, Kathleen McNeill, wife of a Glaswegian forge master, told the court how she had attended one of Helen's seances at which her sister appeared. Her sister had apparently died a few hours prior to the seance taking place, after an operation, and news of her death could not have been known to Helen. But Albert, Helen Duncan's guide, announced that she had just passed over. At a later seance, a few years later Mrs McNeill's own late father walked out of the seance cabinet and came up close to her to display his single eye, which he had in his earthly life. Also, the sailor who spoke about the sinking of HMS *Hood* had materialized as a full body.

Sceptics pointed out that plain cheesecloth has a similar colour to ectoplasm as well as a light airy texture so it would be easy to mould.

Kathleen Goligher, an Irish medium who was highly sought after for her physical mediumship skills in the 1920s, was eventually exposed by paranormal writer Hereward Carrington in his book *The Story of Psychic Science* (1930), claiming that the photographs of Goligher in seances were highly dubious, despite an engineer, William Jackson Crawford, researching her for six years and pronouncing her genuine. Eventually, the physicist Edmund Edward Fournier d'Albe investigated Goligher's mediumship using strict controls and determined that she was indeed a fraud. He had held 20 sittings with Goligher, but she was unable to reproduce any of the extraordinary feats done under Crawford's observations. It was believed she used muslin to simulate ectoplasm.

Ectoplasm has not been found inside the human body, for example during an autopsy, and only small samples have ever been taken for laboratory analysis but they later vanish in the containers, including samples taken by Harry Price. It is as though this material is supported in some way by the presence of spirits in a seance room and at all other times, it retreats or remains hidden in the bodies of the medium and the sitters. This suggests we may all have ectoplasm inside of us, but it will only be available should the need for it arise. Perhaps when ordinary people see solid spirits in their own homes, this ectoplasm is being drawn from the witness without them knowing. For example, could Jan in Chapter 1 have actually been the source of the ectoplasm potentially used by the Native American spirit guide emerging from her airing cupboard?

In theory, the same substance could have been drawn from everyone in the Old Bailey courtroom where Helen's trial took place. During the trial she did offer to hold a full seance in court to prove her psychic abilities to the jury. Had a demonstration been permitted to go ahead, then all manner of people could have potentially come through her mediumship and proved their continued existence beyond death. Unfortunately, after discussing it with the jury the judge decided that a seance would not be permitted. The judge at first declined to consult the jury 'with matters of that sort', but then relented; however, the jury rejected the idea of a full-blown seance demonstration.

AFTER PRISON

Imprisonment did not deter Helen from continuing to demonstrate her abilities as a psychic medium. Indeed, many eyewitnesses who saw her after her release from prison after the war in 1944 and had some astounding stories to relate. One man described in a letter his experiences of Chinese spirit guides manifesting complete with long beards, and mothers coming back as solid forms to visit their sons, only to disappear as a mist into the floor. One witness recalled seeing their sister, who had died in a fire, as well as a Scottish Highlander who came out from behind the seance curtain with his bagpipes and a Highland pony that appeared to be nodding its head! The spirit pony alone would have been an incredibly difficult fake to manage without anyone noticing.

'UNCLE ALBERT'

As for Helen's spirit guide Albert, he was reportedly very open to being investigated, allowing himself to be photographed, inviting people to examine spirit forms more closely and even giving permission for samples of ectoplasm to be taken and studied. These specimens of ectoplasm were at first placed in distilled water at the request of 'Albert' to prevent disintegration by members of London Psychic Research Centre. Later they were taken back to the lab in London and were hermetically sealed and preserved in alcohol. Albert also gave permission to a Dr Rust to examine him in his fully materialized state at the London Psychic Research Centre in 1931 and even joked that Dr Rust would be able to tell the others that he was 'all man'. Many people claimed that Albert was actually Helen dressed in men's clothes, but he was measured at 6 ft 4 in (1.93 m) while Helen was only around 5 ft 4 in (1.63 m). Albert was Helen's spirit guide until her death in 1956. As Helen lay dying, he is said to have come through to some of her friends, saying, 'We are taking Mrs Duncan home. She has well earned her rest.'

It's my opinion that there was clearly something very remarkable about Helen Duncan and unfortunately the toils of war would unfairly tarnish her name with the words 'fake' and 'witch'. For me, nothing could be further from the truth. Perhaps the greater injustice is that no one in the British establishment seems to have considered that her ability could have served a higher purpose. Her skills could have been used not only to help defeat the forces of National Socialism that were wreaking such havoc and misery at the time she was prosecuted, but for the greater good of mankind in countless other ways.

The continuing fascination with the paranormal and spiritualism meant that even later in her life, Helen was still sought after as a highly regarded medium despite having been imprisoned during World War II. Some photographs of her have been used to discredit her abilities. For example, an Australian magazine wanted to illustrate what a materialized spirit in a physical seance might actually look like. A photographer placed some poor-quality papier mache dolls in a studio setting with Helen pretending to go into a trance. Of course, she was a little naïve in agreeing to participate. However, there are also some really compelling photos showing her guide Albert coming out from behind the curtain.

'ENTERTAINMENT PURPOSES ONLY'

Today, television shows featuring spirit mediums and psychics are routinely flagged as 'for entertainment purposes only', which means that the information given out should not be taken too seriously by viewers. Why is this? Most likely it's to avoid legal responsibility because it is remotely possible that someone might take a medium's predictions literally and act on them in a way that causes harm to themselves or others.

These considerations aside, do today's well-known TV mediums like John Edward and Tony Stockwell provide any greater evidence of an afterlife? TV mediumship tends to show demonstrations only at a clairvoyant level rather than showing physical materializations, which is not compelling enough to convince sceptics that there is indeed a spiritual life after our physical death.

It is a great pity that Helen Duncan is not alive today, so we could witness her holding an actual seance live on television, using modern lighting technology. A fully materialized spirit recorded on camera in a room, with several witnesses to attest there is no manipulation going on, would be very strong evidence, even for the most sceptical. Having said this, in our increasingly polarized world, where artificial intelligence is blurring the boundaries between what is real and fake to an alarming degree, many people would probably still find it impossible to believe the evidence of their own eyes.

CHAPTER FIVE

AMAZING READINGS AND HELP FROM ETS?

I write from a viewpoint that the physical world we all inhabit may not be the only plane of existence, and there may be others to experience in this life and after its end. While I don't personally require concrete and direct proof that supernatural beings like spirits, faeries and extra-terrestrials exist, I find the prospect of glimpsing the 'other' to be incredibly life-affirming. In this chapter we'll look at some of the occasions when the spirit world has made itself known here in ways that are astonishing.

True psychic mediumship does more than offer accurate information to sitters. It embodies the feeling that a real intelligence is acting behind the scenes, as if those in spirit have quite knowingly put the right people in the right place at the right time, because the messages conveyed are so far beyond the ordinary. This chapter illustrates some instances where, for me, mediums cannot have engineered what happened. We'll also consider a lawyer's thoughts about such evidence and consider how learning more about UFOs might also be connected to the idea of an afterlife.

ONE WINIFRED AND TWO CHRIS HAYES

True readings are often done in a very spontaneous way, despite the background planning that goes into putting on such an event. In 2018 Alex Geddes, a TV technician, attended a demonstration of mediumship by Southampton-based medium Ross Bartlett, and described it as a privileged experience he was never to forget. Two seats were reserved for Alex and his wife, but these were not paid for in advance by credit card, just reserved as first name only. The reading occurred in Ruislip, a suburb of west London.

Arriving late, Alex and his wife were greeted at the door by a friendly man in a white shirt and tie, who pointed them to some empty seats. Alex had only just taken off his coat as Ross was completing his first reading with another audience member, when Ross looked over to Alex and said, 'I want to come to the gentleman to my left,' while pointing directly at him. Alex gulped, feeling a little guilty as he was the late arrival, and Ross continued, 'I have a Winifred who wants to speak with you.' Alex did not know of anyone called Winifred, but Ross insisted she was definitely with Alex on this reading.

Perplexed, Alex listened as Ross went on, 'Winifred is known to your brother Phil.' Alex confirmed he does have a brother Phil, who happened to have an interest in family history. Ross then announced the arrival of an Edward, who was a partner of Winifred. This confused Alex even more as he couldn't remember anyone in his family with the name Edward. Ross mentioned a Welsh man who Alex identified as his grandad, Bob. Ross spoke about Alex having a large and mostly male family (he had four brothers), and correctly mentioned the names Russell and Simon, as well as Philip.

Next, Ross told Alex that Winifred looks in on a 'Mary' from time to time and Alex replied that Mary was the name of his daughter. Nobody in that room knew Alex apart from the event organizer who reserved his seats and, obviously, Alex's wife. Ross could not have known Alex's name: there was no advanced credit card booking or even any paper tickets with names on them because attendees paid cash on the door.

But something amazing happened that even made Ross doubt the information that was coming through. He told Alex, 'I don't know what is being indicated here, but let's go for it'. He pointed to the friendly white-shirted man at the entrance, saying his name was Chris Hayes and then continued, seeming to pause as the information came to him, 'Winifred says that Mary [Alex's daughter] is also connected to a man by the same name of Chris Hayes!' An amazed Alex announced that indeed his daughter Mary had been dating a man for two years, and he was indeed called Chris Hayes! The audience clapped, just as amazed as Alex at Ross identifying this incredible connection between Alex, his daughter, her boyfriend, and the man on the ticket desk.

This could be seen as the spirit world taking quick advantage of the serendipity of this situation to help Ross establish a connection with Alex. He arrived late to the demonstration and could easily have missed the whole thing, so maybe the spirit world didn't want to let this opportunity go and got Ross to call over to Alex while Winifred's energy was still there. They cleverly used the advantage of having a Chris Hayes who was in the room and connected it back to the other Chris Hayes that Alex knew of.

WINIFRED AND EDWARD REVEALED

What of the mysterious 'Winifred', who was bringing most of this information through to Ross? The day after the reading Alex called some family members to ask if they knew about a Winifred. Most had no idea who she could have been except for one older relative, an aunt. She told Alex that Winifred was in fact his late Auntie Doris! Her name was actually Winifred Doris but she didn't like her first name and switched to using her middle name; as a result everyone in the family called her Doris and never referred to her as Winifred, even after her death. Alex himself had grown up knowing her as Auntie Doris, the name by which she was known in the family.

Ross the medium had said that Winifred's spirit was present at the reading with that of her partner, Edward. Auntie Doris did have a husband, Uncle Ted, and Ted is of course short for Edward. Alex did not make that connection instantly because at that point he had no idea who Winifred was, let alone her husband. Alex later checked with his younger brother Phil, who confirmed he had taken some photos of Auntie Doris's grave, backing up what Winifred had told Ross in the reading about 'being known' to him.

For Alex this was no cold reading, when a supposed psychic or medium makes vague, unverifiable statements. In my own view it was very precise in terms of names and things that happened that were beyond conscious knowledge. Ross was confident that he was correct, even though the strange 'Chris Hayes' connection seemed to give him pause for a few moments. The name change to Winifred was something that the spirit world had decided to do, I believe, to get Alex to put in some work and connect with people in his family. Although 'Winifred' did not exist in Alex's world, Auntie Doris was apparently very much there with him.

As this account shows, Ross is particularly talented at bringing through information relating to spirits' names and identities. He mentioned nothing about how the spirit passed, whereas some mediums seem to be extremely adept at this. Quite why this is so, is not entirely clear. It is interesting to consider whether Doris' information would have come through differently, had it been filtered through another medium. I think each medium could have a different way of interpreting the messages, feelings, images, smells and sounds they receive. Alex's Auntie Doris may have had something very different to say had she come through the mediumship of Philip Kinsella, who is based in Bedfordshire. Philip has a specific way of tuning into a spirit communicator and can give very clear details of their passing.

SHARK ATTACK

Philip has said that one passing in particular made a lasting impact on him. During a private reading in 2010, Philip received the last earthly life impressions from a spirit as mental images. While doing clairvoyance, through the spirit communicator Philip could see black water all around and heard the sound of men frantically shouting above. There was the swift movement of a large grey creature breaching the surface of the water and coming up towards the communicator with its jaws open wide and its eyes white and rolled back. Then came the devastating and fatal bite. In one swift movement his leg was gone and the Great White shark was falling backwards into the water, surrounded by blood mixed with seawater. Philip came back to the awareness of the room where he was giving the reading. The message's recipient sat there, open-mouthed in shock that Philip had managed to describe the last moments of his friend, who had died five years earlier in a shark attack off the coast of Australia.

The sitter Paul explained that he and a group of other young men were larking about in a boat and this turned into a game of dare, with them taking turns to jump into the water, as if they were baiting the sharks to get them to come closer. They knew sharks had been spotted in these waters but wanted to feel the thrill of being next to such awesome but dangerous creatures. It went terribly wrong. The sitter said they saw a shark coming close while one of the friends was still in the water and they were trying to haul him out, but the shark leaped out of the water and grabbed his leg as they were lifting him out. Sadly, he died on the boat soon after, due to massive blood loss. Yet here was that very same young man, five years later, coming through the mental mediumship of Philip, and explaining in graphic detail how he passed.

BARNUM STATEMENTS

Could Philip somehow have deduced enough information about this traumatic event from the young man to guess he had seen a shark attack, and then made up the details? Sceptics often accuse mediums of teasing out 'unknowable' personal information by doing cold readings, also called 'Barnum statements'. This is where a medium says something very general, such as 'You have a great need for other people to like and admire you,' or 'You have a great deal of unused capacity, which you have not turned to your advantage.' It was named after P.T. Barnum, a great showman of the 19th century who coined the phrase, 'There is a sucker born every minute.'

There is some debate over who invented the term 'Barnum statement', but it was first documented in 1948 by the American professor of psychology Bertram R. Forer during experiments with his students using personality tests. But the name Barnum stuck with this type of personality statement test, suggesting that people agreeing with them must be foolish 'suckers'. Also called the 'Forer effect', the idea is that humans are always looking for meaning so they tend to extract personal information from a general statement in order to validate it.

True mediums do not use this kind of approach; they are just receivers of messages, which they have to pass on to the recipient. I have personally seen Philip do many demonstrations in front of a live audience, including some I have organized, and I can say with certainty that he has no prior knowledge of people who would attend. What's more, I knew many of the people Philip read for in the room so I don't believe he can be accused of inviting 'stooges' or paid plants to be in the audience. He brings through names of loved ones and will often go into very precise detail about how the person died. It's difficult to say how a general statement could possibly result in his cold reading that the sitter had witnessed a shark attack. After all, very few people have ever encountered a shark, and shark attacks are even more rare.

Phineas Taylor Barnum was one of the greatest showmen of 19th-century America.

At another of Philip's demonstrations in 2011, he described in great detail the dress worn by the spirit of a deceased woman who was coming through. Philip was picking up a mother of the daughter who was in the audience. She was buried in it because it was her favourite dress. The spirit also mentioned a recent family wedding that she had visited and observed. She reported that the wedding cake had been knocked off the table by children running around – which had happened! Once again, these are quite specific statements as opposed to generalizations like 'You are shy in front of strangers,' or 'You like nice clothes.'

TRIAL BY TELEVISION

In 2010, a reading based on Barnum statements was actually put to the test with a sceptical professor of psychology and world-famous Scottish medium Gordon Smith, when both appeared on the UK television programme *This Morning*. The psychologist claimed that all mediums use Barnum-type general statements in their readings and he challenged Gordon Smith to a live phone-in, where viewers were given the opportunity to have a reading on air with both himself and Gordon. Neither man was told the names of the callers or any details about them; all they had to go on was the voice of the caller, who would then either confirm or deny the information given by the psychologist and Gordon. The caller would just say hello and then Gordon and the psychologist would proceed with the reading.

All the callers said that they felt that Gordon Smith gave the more accurate readings whereas the psychologist's messages were too general. After the live programme went to a commercial break, Gordon and the psychologist both went outside the studio for a cigarette. The psychologist allegedly said to Gordon, 'You made me look a fool in there.' Gordon looked at him, astonished, and replied, 'You made yourself look a fool!'

'I AM HERE!'

There are numerous accounts of Gordon's extraordinary abilities. At one London demonstration in 2011, Gordon informed an Asian woman who was sitting by herself that he was bringing her mother through. He proceeded to give her some messages from her late mother, one of which was to watch out for the woman's brother! She said the woman's brother, although a nice chap, was quite manipulative and would try and wrap her around his little finger. The woman nodded in agreement at this and said, 'Thank you.'

Then, suddenly, Gordon's jaw dropped and he held his hand to his mouth and gulped in horror. He said, 'Oh my goodness, I have just been told, your brother is here tonight!' He said the spirit world was now pointing her brother out to him and Gordon correctly picked out an Asian man in the farthest corner of the room. This man put up his hand, smiled and waved and said, 'Yes, that is me, boss! I am here!' and was laughing at poor Gordon, who looked like he wanted the ground to swallow him up.

It seemed that this man had decided before the event not to sit next to his sister because he knew people might assume they were together and so he made a conscious decision to sit right at the back of the church, where he was much less likely to be spotted. But the spirit world apparently knew all this and highlighted it to Gordon. Again, there were no Barnum-type statements made by Gordon before his message to the woman.

A sceptic would probably argue that the man was planted there in advance by Gordon Smith to make him look good. But if the man was a so-called stooge, he would probably want to be paid for this service and could also have come forward later to say that he is was working for Gordon – along with all the countless other supposed plants that must go along to all those mediumship demonstrations that are happening, if the sceptics are correct. To date, I'm not aware of anyone who has come forward with an admission like this.

A RESEARCHER SEES FOR HIMSELF

The US-based writer and reincarnation researcher Stephen Sakellarios conducted his own research on mediums including Gordon Smith and the famous American medium John Edward. Having watched many of their demonstrations on YouTube, he concluded that either they were what they said they were – mediums receiving communications from another world – or they had paid stooges in the audience pretending to accept their messages, and then used clever editing to present their abilities to the greatest effect.

Stephen then decided to do further research by going to one of John Edward's live demonstrations. He was seated quite close to John Edward when he came out into the audience to try and pinpoint the person who was the intended recipient for his reading. John Edward said he could see a 'blackness in the chest'. Stephen continued his account, noting that 'these two or three related ladies didn't respond, because it had been lung cancer which had spread to the brain, so they thought it wasn't a literal match. I was seated on the aisle, perhaps a third of the way back, in an audience of about 3,000 people – a big room. [John] Edward walked down the aisle, stopping right directly next to me, with his back turned toward me. He pointed directly at these ladies and said, "It's right in here." No prior guesses – no large area.'

John Edward was drawn to a woman who was sitting close to Stephen, and he gave her some very accurate facts about her late mother, who he said was coming through. The woman became quite emotional and began to break down and cry during the reading. After the reading had concluded, and John Edward closed the show, everyone started to put their coats on and leave. Stephen then added, 'The reason the lady was crying, was that she had lived on the West Coast [the demonstration was happening on the East Coast of America] and she hadn't been able to make it to say goodbye to her mother. Edward picked up on that theme as well, not too surprisingly.'

Stephen looked over at this woman who had the last reading and he noticed that she was still crying, even some ten minutes after it had finished. He concluded that she could not have been a stooge, because they would have stopped the acting the moment the reading had finished. Further research by the author has indicated that no stooges have come forward to sell their stories in the papers or TV or gone to people like the late magician James Randi, who was keen to expose all mediums as frauds.

THE SOCIAL MEDIA ARGUMENT

Social media channels such as Facebook are often cited as the information source that supposed fake mediums, or all mediums, go to for personal details to use in their readings. This does beg the question, how did they manage before the internet arrived? One young researcher recently produced a video on social media explaining how he had gone to a medium and the medium had correctly described, among other things, how his grandfather had died. Then he brought in a friend (who happened to be a magician) who showed him how easy it was for a medium, or anyone, to go online and buy a copy of a death certificate. (In the UK death certificates list the cause of death and details like where it happened and the deceased person's job.)

How viable is this in reality? Each time a medium has to come up with a cause of death, they would have to purchase a death certificate, possibly for a lot of different recipients in a public demonstration. Not forgetting all the other information they have to research and maybe purchase from different sources beforehand. With all that expense in money and time for every single reading, it's doubtful the medium would be able to cover their overheads. After all, one of the main criticisms of mediums is that they must be in it for the money. I wonder how it could really be worth it?

In a public setting, it would be no small feat for a medium to try and retain all the details of who, what and why, for each person they read for. The idea of using general cold reading statements also contradicts the argument that mediums always pre-research personal information on websites and social media. Can the sceptics have it both ways? It's also interesting to note that Barnum statements tend to be positive, rather than broad statements about things or people we don't like or characteristics we don't admire. The next account illustrates a case where a reaction to a message was negative, but still compelling.

'WE DON'T WANT TO HEAR FROM HIM'

Most people go to see a psychic or medium either because they are interested in the paranormal or want to connect with a loved one who has passed over. Some want so desperately to hear from, say, their late mum or dad that they may well try to fit the information coming through to themselves. Sometimes, though, things happen very differently. I was at the close of a demonstration in Hertfordshire with two talented mediums. Both thanked their audience and went off stage. Suddenly one of them, Daniel Turner, came back on stage and said, 'Hold on one moment please.' He informed the audience that he had just received one last message to pass on, indicating it was for three middle-aged women who were sitting together at the back of the hall.

The medium said, 'I believe I have your father here.' Before he could say any more, all three of the women shouted out, 'We don't want to hear from him!' Although he was quite surprised to hear this, the medium said he understood their viewpoint but said that their father really wanted to come through to say sorry. They still refused to accept anything to do with their father. But the medium continued and relayed a message about their father being sorry for something he did, indicating he was not very nice to his daughters during his earthly life. Now he was on the other side, he had become more aware of just how much damage he had caused them, and it seemed as though he was almost pleading with the medium to pass on his regret and apology.

The women remained silent and listened but said nothing in return. We can't know the reason for this; maybe they didn't want to accept that this was the spirit of their father, or it was still too painful for them to remember and admit, especially in a public setting.

STRANDED ON LINDISFARNE

In 2019, Jackie Wright, a fantastic medium who hails from the north-east of England, gave a reading to a woman regarding her late husband. He was described as a very smartly dressed fellow, and felt that she was holding a large steering wheel in her hands. The woman confirmed that her husband did indeed drive coaches, which have bigger steering wheels than cars. Next, Jackie said she was getting information about the husband having once broken down in his coach at the end of a bridge by the Isle of Lindisfarne, and that it was quite a few hours until the roadside recovery service arrived. The man's wife confirmed all this was exactly right.

This was very precise information that could only apply to one person in the room. At the end of the demonstration, the woman was heard to say quietly to her friend, 'Good job she didn't mention my present husband in that reading!' To me, that reaction suggested she was highly unlikely to be a plant in the audience. In any case, the fact of a coach breaking down is such a minor personal occurrence, it was unlikely anyone outside the woman's close family would have even known about it.

'MR MEDIUM'

Gordon Higginson (1918–93) was another brilliant medium and spiritualist who was known as 'Mr Medium' and is still regarded by many as one of the best in the business. In his heyday he was also president of the Spiritualists National Union. People were reportedly transfixed as he gave out one accurate piece of information after another, sometimes doing two readings at the same time with people sitting at opposite ends of the room!

Gordon's parents were also mediums and they trained him from an early age; at three years old he was already sitting in spiritual development circles. At age 12 he would have to stand on a crate in a spiritualist church so he could be seen and give out messages to those in attendance. One day while he was doing this, a car pulled up outside and the driver threw a brick through the window of the church – it crashed down beside young Gordon, who was naturally very startled. His mother, who was there, told him sternly, 'Don't stop, carry on!' Young Gordon did as he was told and managed to complete his demonstration successfully. He became known as 'The Wonder Boy' due to his accuracy and his blossoming abilities. Gordon went on to develop physical mediumship skills as well as mental mediumship.

WARDROBE MALFUNCTION

At one demonstration of mental mediumship, Gordon came to a man near the front and said to him, 'You sir, the coat you are wearing here tonight, is not the original coat you came out in. You originally came out in a different coat than the one you have on now and got in your car, and decided to go back in and change your coat. You went into your bedroom, threw the original coat on to your bed and got out the one you are now wearing from your wardrobe. You came here in a small red sports car and my helpers [spirit guides] have just gone down to the multi-story car park below us, and come back with your registration number containing the letters of "PYE".' Gordon could not quite get the other two letters, but managed to repeat the last few of the number plate. The man agreed that his number plate did contain those letters and that everything Gordon had said actually happened only a few hours earlier!

Gordon then went on and gave out people's phone numbers, home addresses, what the inside of their houses looked like, and personal details of loved ones that were giving him this information. These were not vague statements, or guessing, or body language readings. In fact, when Gordon did readings in a theatre or large hall, many of the people he read for were at the back or in the upper circles and out of sight. He would often call out to the people further back, to prove to critics that he was not just reading body language.

TOUCHING ECTOPLASM

Gordon would often give mental mediumship demonstrations while in a trance, with various guides speaking through him, and he also performed physical mediumship in more strictly controlled conditions. He was also able to do healing sessions while in trance. In 1972 the newspaper *Psychic News* reported on one of his physical mediumship seances at Stansted Hall in Essex, which was witnessed by 80 people. As outlined in the following paragraphs, the report included detailed eyewitness testimony from a woman who saw ectoplasm pour from Gordon's nose, mouth and, quite surprisingly for her, his navel.

The journalist reported that Gordon's child spirit guide, Cuckoo, materialized at his side in the red light, and was then seen to disappear and then reappear. At one point the ectoplasm draped like a transparent curtain through which audience members on each side of the room could clearly see each other. The child spirit materialized outside the seance cabinet beside Gordon and stood there – she was a small girl, just over 3 ft (90 cm) in height. She said, 'Watch me, I'm going down' and then vanished down into the floor. 'Here I come again,' she said, rising up from the floorboards!

Eileen Garrod sat at the left of the cabinet and her husband, Stanley, who was to the right, controlled the red lights. Both Eileen and her husband helped with the event, and might not be the most reliable witnesses. Eileen asked if it was possible for the guides to drape ectoplasm over her extended hand and the spirits were apparently happy to oblige. As she held it firmly between finger and thumb, Eileen reported that it felt quite dry and was 'like cotton voile in texture, soft but firm' and also 'a compressed mass gradually becoming smooth, hard and firm'. Other spirit guides said they would demonstrate how the ectoplasm formed itself into shapes and a mass of ectoplasm poured like a thick folded bunch over Gordon's hand, said Eileen. She continued, 'As my hand was taken and placed on top of this, I tried to feel through it gently with my fingers, as if squeezing an orange. It was crisp, dry and emitted a crunchy sound rather like dried snow or starched cotton folds being gathered in my hand.'

'I WANT MY WIFE'

More demonstrations followed where the ectoplasm was observed flowing out of Gordon's mouth and solar plexus areas (including the navel) on to the floor and then spirit visitors from the other side began to come through with messages for their loved ones on this side. It was reported that a voice coming from Gordon's seance cabinet said, 'I want my wife Margaret' and then the materialized figure of a man emerged to greet his wife, who was sitting in the audience. The sitter Margaret was quite understandably overwhelmed by this first-ever contact with her husband's spirit.

A Mrs Catchpole was the next person to hear from a relative who had passed over, according to the report. The first was the spirit of her late husband, then an elderly woman materialized. 'It's Mother,' said the spirit form. 'Today is a special day, isn't it?' Mrs Catchpole later confirmed it was indeed her mother's birthday. The presence at the demonstration of journalists from *Psychic News* makes this account even more fascinating. Journalists, after all, are professional sceptics who would be the first to cry foul if they had suspected any trickery was going on. Yet they reported the events as they saw them and followed

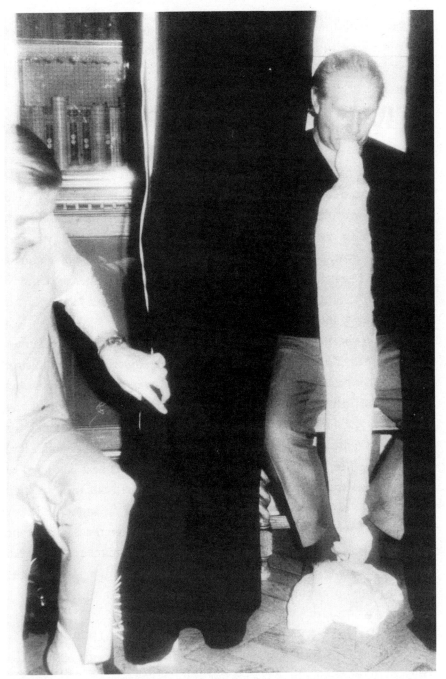

Medium Gordon Higginson with the supposed ectoplasm emerging from his mouth.

Gordon's work for most of his life, never once reporting anything other than phenomena that appeared entirely genuine.

MEDIUMSHIP AND THE POLICE

Various police forces around the world have on occasion asked for help from mediums to try and solve murders when there is just not enough information to go on. While law enforcement agencies clearly prefer not to discuss it, occasionally a television documentary will feature a clairvoyant receiving information that helps solve the crime. Sometimes, the spirit of the murdered person can come through and relay in great detail how they died and who the killer is.

Tricia Robertson, psychical researcher and author of *Things You Can Do When You're Dead!: True Accounts of After Death Communication*, suggested what she thought was the most convincing evidence of after-death communication that she has personally witnessed. A Glaswegian mother called Tricia pleaded with her for help, as her poor daughter had been murdered and the local police had nothing to go on. Tricia collected a few objects that had belonged to the murdered young woman, which her mother had put into a sealed envelope. She took the envelope to a few mediums she knew, and they could only give her small snippets of information. Frustrated, she approached another medium, but he was reluctant to get involved. However, Tricia insisted that he should at least try to tune into possible information that might come forth.

'THIS GIRL HAS BEEN MURDERED'

The medium placed his hand on the envelope and immediately looked Tricia in the eyes, in a light trance-like state. He then said, 'This girl has been murdered and she misses her three cats! She is telling me, she has two tattoos on her chest in the shape of two intertwined hearts, and one on her left arm in the shape of a rose. Her boyfriend was the first one to find out she was dead and phoned to tell her mum.'

Next, recounted Tricia, the spirit of the murdered young woman informed the medium that she was in Cornton Vale prison in Stirling when she was younger. She then said she was killed by two men and gave their names as well as an address connected with the murder in Glasgow. In total, the medium gave Tricia 29 specific points relating to this victim and the conditions around her murder. He also relayed that her mother had moved the photo of her murdered daughter from the mantelpiece to the TV set that very day. Two days later Tricia, who had never been in the young woman's house before, was visiting the mother. The first thing she noticed was the photo of a young girl on the TV set. 'Is that your daughter?' Tricia asked her. 'Yes, it is,' said the mother, 'I moved her photo to the TV set two days ago.'

Tricia gave the mother 23 out of the 29 specific points made by the medium; she felt some of the information given to her was too personal or possibly upsetting for the young woman's mother, and not really of any additional help to the police. Of those 23 points, the mother confirmed every single one as correct. Again this cannot be explained by cold body reading or Barnum statements, as Tricia didn't know any of the facts to be able to confirm anything until after she had shown the envelope to the last medium.

Even the most sceptical person would find this account hard to dismiss. Maybe the best argument they could put forward is the medium and the researcher conspired somehow in order to boost book sales. However, this experience was personally very convincing for Tricia, and at that point her motive for the reading was to help the police, which was far more time-sensitive than writing a book. The information was passed to the relevant police force but to date no one has been charged, even though it is thought that police strongly suspect the two men that were named in the reading.

A LAWYER'S POINT OF VIEW

If you took the evidence for the afterlife and presented it to a judge in a theoretical court case, I believe that judge would have to rule that there is indeed an afterlife. This is also the opinion of Victor Zammit, a retired lawyer from Australia. Victor and his wife Wendy run a website titled 'A lawyer presents the evidence for the afterlife' (www.victorzammit.com) and co-authored the book *What Happens When We Die? A Lawyer Presents the Evidence for the Afterlife.*

Victor describes himself as 'an open-minded sceptic' and says that after more than 30 years of serious research, he and his wife came to the conclusion that there is a great body of evidence that 'taken as a whole, absolutely and unqualifiedly prove the case for an afterlife or spirit world'. As part of their research, Victor and Wendy attended one particular medium's seances over a five-year period, witnessing more than 100 materialization seances in detail. The medium, David Thompson, demonstrates physical mediumship in Australia and around the world, and Victor and Wendy concluded that his mediumship is entirely genuine.

Victor makes the point that afterlife evidence is hard to come by because of the bias shown by scientists and materialists (who believe that nothing exists unless it has a solid material form). In addition, sceptics tend to receive more media coverage than those who say the afterlife exists.

Victor and Wendy also raise some truly fascinating questions around what would happen in the event of concrete proof for the afterlife. Once it is established that an afterlife awaits, then personal responsibility – how one goes about in one's life – becomes far more important because the afterlife is a place of self-judgement. We are informed by spirits, for example, that war does not exist in their afterlife. If this was accepted by most people, it would naturally follow that political and military aggression would be questioned far more severely in our reality. In addition, people here would seek every opportunity to communicate with the next life and seek answers to questions about existence, love and morality. This could destabilize major organized religions as millions of people turn to the dead for answers, something they have broadly speaking rejected, labelling it as dealing with demonic forces. They, along with humanity as a whole, would surely have to adapt to a new world paradigm.

Of course, the issue here is what needs to happen to establish, as Victor Zammit puts it, that the afterlife awaits. In the next chapters we consider the roles of science and organized religion in providing acceptable proof and normalizing the concept of a spirit world. In the meantime, is it possible that assistance could be found in another paranormal sphere?

CONNECTING UFOS AND THE AFTERLIFE

A few open-minded religious groups and people are comfortable with the idea of investigating and proving the afterlife exists, such as those religious individuals that worked with the direct voice medium Leslie Flint (discussed in Chapter 6). When it comes to UFO phenomena, the powers that be are fully aware of their existence and know a lot about what and who these beings are. We, the public, are still only receiving scraps from the table of knowledge. In the UFO field the ongoing question is when will 'disclosure', the term used for announcing official UFO information in full to the public, finally happen? Many people believe that those hiding it have run out of road (or maybe, in this case, runway) and cannot hide this knowledge for much longer. If that is the case, and the true nature of UFOs, flying saucers, aliens or ETs is made known to the public, it is my guess that in due course the case for a continued existence beyond the life of this Earth would also become common and accepted knowledge.

The reason I think this would inevitably happen is that as more information about UFOs and their occupants becomes official, then we would learn from certain races of the spiritual side of life in greater depth. Many contactees, or in today's terms 'experiencers' – those people who claim to have had contact with some of these alien races – have described more positive encounters with extra-terrestrial beings known as the 'Nordics'.

NORDIC ALIENS

Nordic aliens are said to look human in appearance, with a passing resemblance to the typical features of people from Scandinavian countries. They have been described as tall and pale, with light hair and large foreheads. From descriptions given by those that have come across them, these 'Nordics' tend to be telepathic in nature but also a very spiritual and gentle-natured race, as if they are highly evolved versions of humans. They seem to be aware of other dimensions and afterlife environments, and also the possibility of reincarnation, where one might live many different types of life, with episodes of being in a spirit world between those lives. If they were given an open platform and invited to do so, the Nordics might widen our knowledge in many areas, which as mentioned previously would create a paradigm shift in thinking about Earth's evolution.

The connection between the afterlife and other worlds may have already been witnessed in this dimension. UFOs made an appearance in the famous 'Scole experiments' of the 1990s, in which a group of psychical researchers and mediums jointly held a series of seances in the basement of a house in Norfolk in an attempt to definitively prove an existence after death. During one of their seances, a small UFO about 2 ft long materialized and flew around the room for ten minutes with lights ablaze. The Scole experiments were also said to have resulted in grey, alien-type beings projecting their images on to photographs.

PRISON PLANET?

Another interesting theory suggests that humanity is actually imprisoned on our planet, through a rigid control of knowledge – despite the advent of the internet. This theory was promoted by Alex Jones via his website around 2006. One self-described 'out-of-body explorer' raised this possibility when calling a US radio show, where the guest was Robert Monroe, author of the classic work, *Journeys out of the Body*. The caller spoke about his own attempts at leaving his corporeal body. Following Monroe's advice, he managed to leave his body on many occasions and, on one such journey, to have floated away from Earth and landed on another unknown planet. The caller then claimed to have encountered other beings there, who could see his etheric body, and asked him where he had travelled from. He replied that he had come from Earth and they seemed to know of it, saying it was known as a prison planet!

Elsewhere, Victor and Wendy Zammitt gathered a wealth of information for their book to show that many respected scientists and doctors have witnessed and signed testaments saying they have experienced proof of life after death. Victor and Wendy cite a number of cases they have uncovered from around the world, notably Brazil, where psychic phenomena seem to be in abundance and from where many UFO cases are reported. Could Brazil be a source of portals or might there be other forces at play there? For example, could Brazilian conditions actually enable daylight spirit materializations?

RADIATION BELTS

Victor Zammit writes about 'materializations taking place in daylight in the presence of hundreds of hard-core sceptics'. That these materializations were allegedly happening in daylight is very interesting. Most of the physical spirit materializations mentioned previously in this book took place in only infrared light, because of the sensitivity of ectoplasm to daylight. Many mediums and so-called psychic surgeons have come from Brazil. Taking a sceptical view, there may simply be a

The paranormal phenomena produced by Brazilian medium Carmine Mirabelli were observed by hundreds of witnesses.

lot of people there who see the opportunity to jump aboard the psychic 'gravy train'. But maybe there is another explanation that lies in the specific conditions there: namely, the Van Allen Belts. These belts of highly charged radioactive particles are trapped by Earth's magnetic field and surround our planet, at around 600 miles to 20,000 miles above the Earth's surface. They prevent most of the Sun's radiation hitting the Earth.

However, in an area known as the South Atlantic Anomaly some of the radiation manages to seep through the belts and dips down to about 100 miles above Earth, including most of Brazil. Researcher Robert Hulse discovered that a solar flare occurred during the materialization of his deceased wife. He speculated that she may have used those particles of energy to help manifest herself. Perhaps the extra-charged particles hitting the South Atlantic through this anomaly might account for the extra phenomena in Brazil. As already suggested, this could also be responsible for creating portals. While this is pure speculation right now, the spirit guide Seth, who revealed information to American psychic Jane Roberts, spoke about 'co-ordination points' around the world where energy flows through dimensions from one reality to another. Perhaps the deviations in the Van Allen Belts might contribute to the communication between worlds.

In his book Victor Zammit writes about the fascinating case of Brazilian medium Carmine Mirabelli, who is thought to have produced incredible physical phenomena that were witnessed by scientists from around the world (see below). In contrast to the physical mediumship described in earlier chapters here, the 1927 Portuguese-language book *O Medium Mirabelli* contained reports of the phenomena that occurred in broad daylight. Daylight manifestations are harder for sceptics to write off; most accusations of fraud are made against mediums practising materializations in darkened rooms, where it is easier to conceal trickery.

Not only did Carmine Mirabelli produce physical manifestations in natural daylight, up to 60 witnesses stated they saw the phenomena. These included the then-president of Brazil, his secretary of state, as well as two professors of medicine, 72 doctors, 12 engineers, 36 lawyers, 89 'men of public office', 25 military men, 52 bankers, 128 merchants and 22 dentists and even priests. It seems likely that someone on this illustrious list would have been able to spot whether Carmine Mirabelli was a fake. Maybe the atmospheric conditions of the Van Allen radiation belts including the South Atlantic Anomaly aided these manifestations in some way, although we may never know.

A SPECIAL INVESTIGATION

Mirabelli's abilities became the subject of a special investigation committee headed by the president, which interviewed witnesses and further investigated Mirabelli's mediumship. The *Academia de Estudos Psychicos* ('Academy of Psychical Studies') was established in 1927 and divided its investigation into three groups: one dealt with clairvoyant mediumship sessions, the second with automatic writing, and the third group investigated physical phenomena. Forty of the physical mediumship seances were held in daylight and 23 in bright artificial light with Mirabelli tied up in a chair. The seance rooms used for these experiments were searched before and after each session.

Many of the seances and readings were successful but some were failures. It's important to remember that sometimes readings and seances do not produce spirit voices or materializations. This is why, as mentioned earlier, seance organizers will try to raise the energy levels in the room in any way they can. Otherwise it's rather like trying to check signals on a mobile phone when its battery is dead.

When materializations and other events did occur, though, some were reported to be pretty spectacular. In the course of one investigation, while tied to his chair Mirabelli was seen to rise in the air and float up to a height of about 2 m (almost 7 ft) for about two minutes. On another occasion he was with friends at the Da Luz train station when he was seen to dematerialize. Fifteen minutes later a call came from Sao Vicente, a town which is approximately 90 km (55 miles) away, saying that he was there – around two minutes after he had disappeared from Da Luz. Of course, it could be argued that he had accomplices, who hid him at the first station, and other friends were calling from just around the corner pretending to be at Sao Vicente, or that Mirabelli himself hid and made the call from inside the station. But some of the other reports are harder to dismiss.

A SPIRIT CHILD AND A BISHOP

At one of Mirabelli's seances in daylight conditions, a Dr Ganymede de Souza witnessed the materialization of a spirit child – and then confirmed the child was his own daughter who had died two months earlier! The spirit was apparently wearing the same dress in which she was placed in the coffin on the day of her burial. Other witnesses also reported seeing the child appear and then disappear. One, Colonel Octavio Viana, touched the child, and felt her pulse, which was a normal regular rhythm. He also asked her several questions, which she was able to answer with full mental understanding. So, apparently, this was no zombie-like existence.

A photographer managed to take a few photos of the apparition before the materialized child floated around in the air and disappeared. In total her appearance lasted just over half an hour. The next spirit visitor reported to manifest was Bishop Jose de Camargo Barros, who had recently died at sea in a shipwreck. He appeared as a whole body dressed in full bishop's regalia. The bishop spoke to the witness and even permitted a physical examination of his heart, gums, abdomen, hands and fingers, before disappearing.

A SPIRIT PHYSICIAN

At a separate afternoon seance in Santos near São Paulo, 60 witnesses saw the materializing spirit of the deceased Dr Bezerra de Meneses, previously an eminent hospital physician. He apparently spoke through a megaphone to assure everyone of his identify. A number of photographs were taken of him, while two doctors who had known him in his earthly life gave him a thorough examination and declared him to be a normal human in every respect. He shook hands with the witnesses before ascending into the air and slowly dematerializing – feet first, then legs, body and last of all his head.

After Dr Bezerra de Meneses had vanished, the medium Carmine Mirabelli was found to be still tied securely to his chair and seals placed on all the doors and windows of the seance room were intact. Photos from this seance show Mirabelli and the materialized Dr Bezerra de Meneses together on photographic plate, the technology used before film negatives. This account reminds me of the Bible story where Jesus appears to his followers and is then seen rising into the air before vanishing: 'And then, right in front of their eyes, he rose into the air up to heaven', Luke 24:50–52. Could Jesus actually have been a materialized spirit? To me, this makes more sense than a deceased corpse suddenly rising up alive after three days.

According to reports, the deceased Dr Bezerra de Meneses materialized at a seance and was observed by 60 witnesses.

It's strange that there appears to be no motion film of Mirabelli during any of the materialization experiments. Yet we still have images of supposed spirits descending from the sky. In 1927, you could have easily, given that the Brazilian government were investigating him, had the budget to incorporate a few film cameras to capture the phenomena.

In the next chapter we will look more at the attitude of the Christian faith towards spiritualism and in particular an intriguing story about how the Church of England has approached the concept of speaking directly to the spirit world.

CHAPTER SIX

HEARING VOICES, SPIRIT COMMUNICATION AND THE CHURCH

As well as reaching out to our 'normal' world through mediums, it seems that spirits may have long been attempting to make contact by technological means. Sometimes, as the stories below illustrate, these extraordinary events occur through the most mundane items, like a basic wireless radio.

In this chapter we will examine the crucial role of spirit voice recordings in allowing many more people to indirectly experience the 'other side' – whether they consider those spirit voices and noises to be real phenomena or pure chicanery. These stories also illustrate that sometimes the worlds of religion, the paranormal and modern technology intersect in the most surprising ways, and that the Church has not tended to look kindly on those who are interested in engaging in direct communication with the afterlife.

EDISON'S 'WIRELESS TO THE DEAD'

So much of the technology we take for granted today, from the cinematic releases and music enjoyed on our mobile phones to the lighting of our homes, workplaces and streets, can be traced back to Thomas Edison (1847–1931). The phonograph, a sound recording and playback device he patented in 1877, was just one of his many inventions. Surely, given his incredible track record, if Edison had developed a device that allowed for communication with the deceased, it would mean that by now we would be able to chat with deceased friends and loved ones whenever we like via an afterlife-enabled smartphone or some kind of human–spirit video conferencing app? It hasn't happened yet, but it is fascinating to learn that Edison may have at least tried to do exactly that.

'I have been at work for some time building an apparatus to see if it is possible for personalities which have left this earth to communicate with us,' said Edison in a 1920 edition of *The American Magazine*. So if America's greatest inventor was working on an apparatus for communicating with a spirit world, where is it now?

Unfortunately, no plans, schematics or prototypes of his potential device have ever been found to date. Did he actually invent one? In the same year, *Scientific American* magazine also quoted him as saying, 'I have been *thinking* [my emphasis] for some time of a machine or apparatus which could be operated by personalities which have passed on to another existence or sphere.' Edison was interested in developing a communication device using a basic valve system, which was common in the wireless sets and radios of that era. He even suggested that one of his recently deceased employees would be keen to communicate through it!

American inventor Thomas Edison hoped to create a device to communicate with the spirit world.

Could it be possible that a prototype was made but destroyed or hidden, given the nature of such a device? Just as hundreds of Nicolas Tesla's documents and research papers including, supposedly, those for a 'death ray' super weapon, were confiscated by the US government after his death, could Edison's 'wireless to the dead' idea have been effectively classified as top secret after he died? We are not likely to know.

Although no details of an Edison-patented spirit communication device have ever appeared over the years since then, researchers into this area have not ceased trying to forge their own links though technological means. And we will see later in this chapter that those on the other side, including Edison himself, may have tried to reach through to us to help us build communications between one world and another.

FIRST RECORDINGS

One of the earliest recordings on to phonographs or records of voices said to come from the spirit world was made by Reverend Charles Drayton Thomas, who was born in 1868. These might have been recorded on to wax cylinders or soft metal rolls and later transferred to phonograph.

A record of a voice from the spirit world was recorded on phonograph from as early as 1940.

As a Methodist minister in the early 20th century, one might assume that Reverend Thomas would have opposed any communication with spirits of the dead, considering them to be evil spirits or demons. He had a sitting with a medium called Mrs Osborne Leonard in 1917 and later made audio recordings of her in 1940. During one of their sessions together, Thomas found that he had captured on the recording the disembodied voice of his father, in which he received communications from his late father and sister. He went on to devote a large part of his life to investigating claims for the afterlife and spirit communication. How he reconciled this with Christian theological arguments against communication of any kind with the dead is unclear, given that he continued to preach as a minister until his death in 1953.

In fact, Reverend Thomas published a long series of books and articles outlining his experiences with the medium and his received communications. He even introduced a demonstration by the famous medium Leslie Flint when Flint held a mediumship event in London. Reverend Thomas was said to be rigorous in his research, taking a scientific approach to his investigations including copious notes at every sitting. The Society for Psychical Research noted in its journal:

'He kept full and annotated records of his sittings with a care none too frequent among sitters, and generously made these available to other investigators. He also had gramophone records made of some of the communications from his father John ... and presented copies to the Society. The early sitters with Mrs. Leonard were fortunate in having to deal with a medium and control who fully entered into the spirit of scientific investigation, and indeed themselves proposed various methods of research which would provide crucial tests as to whether or not the content of the communications could reasonably be assigned to telepathy.' (Obituary of Reverend C. Drayton Thomas, written by Helen de Gaudrion Salter, used with the kind permission of the Society of Psychical Research).

DIRECT VOICE RECORDINGS

Reverend Thomas managed to capture recordings from a spirit voice in the room that could be heard by all those present using early recording equipment. He may have recorded what is called 'direct voice' – where the spirit voice physically manifests and is audible in the room – rather than EVP ('electronic voice phenomena'), where the spirit voices are not heard until afterwards at the playback of the recording, which is more typical of later research in this area.

Similar recordings were made of Leslie Flint, a British direct voice medium, which is one variation of physical mediumship. Flint was recorded on a portable reel-to-reel tape recorder by Betty Greene and Sydney George Woods for over 20 years, beginning in the early 1950s. Flint claimed to use a separate ectoplasmic 'voice box' that was manufactured by spirits, who then used it to speak by impressing it with their thoughts and making it vibrate.

It's interesting to note that many years later, none other than the now-deceased Reverend Thomas himself made an appearance at one of Leslie Flint's seances and was he himself recorded by the sitters there. Everyone attending Flint's sittings and demonstrations would hear the direct voice manifestations with their own ears and recordings were made 'live' as they were heard coming out of the seance cabinet, where

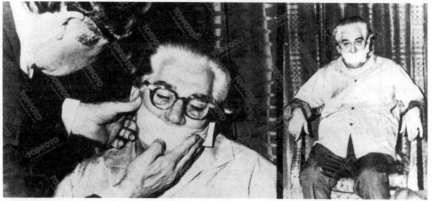

Leslie Flint was one of the leading mediums of his time, but even he was not without his critics.

the spirit-manufactured voice box was levitating. On one occasion the voice box was seen as a mass of ectoplasm floating inside Leslie Flint's seance cabinet. Although the voices appeared to mostly originate inside the seance cabinet that he sometimes sat in, at other times they could be heard in different areas of the room, sometimes directly above the sitter.

Flint was not, however, without his critics. Many sceptics argued against the authenticity of the voices at his seances, the main argument being that many of them sounded similar. However, at his readings and demonstrations the spirit guides themselves explained to the audience that this would happen because one voice box was made for all the communicating spirits. This could be compared to an excellent mimic who still retains the intonations of their original voice, due to the physical makeup of their vocal chords, tongue and mouth. Unlike most other physical mediums, Flint would remain conscious throughout his seances, rather than going into a trance state. He continued his work up until his death in 1994. A fellow medium of Flint's introduced a fascinating new angle on direct voice mediumship – could the spirits themselves be using their own technology to reach into this world?

SPIRIT TECHNOLOGY?

English medium and researcher Leo Bonomo was invited to attend a seance with Flint in 1990. Flint explained to him that the spirits communicating from the other side had to impress their faces into a kind of mask that somehow took their thoughts, amplified them and retransmitted them through to the manifested voice box construction in the seance room.

It is not clear if there was one 'thought mask' device on the other side or many of them, as on other occasions it was reported that many voices could be heard at once. My take on this idea is that there could be a thought mask for each user, rather like a coffee shop full of people with their own mobile phones. The mask itself was not visible to the sitters, although as mentioned, the voice box had been seen in the infrared light typically used by physical mediums like Flint.

Leo Bonomo said he could hear the manifested voice of a gentleman above his head, where the voice box was floating in the dark. A voice identified itself as a Dr Marshall who, before he passed, lived in Southend, to the east of London. Interestingly, the voice moved across the ceiling back and forth, and Leo said that in his clairvoyant vision, he could see this man, with his arms folded around his back, rather official like, pacing up and down dictating his thoughts into the room. So while the voice emanated out of the constructed ectoplasmic voice box, Leo was able simultaneously to see the spirit who was projecting this voice. Maybe the mask device went with them as they moved about the room.

During his conversation with the sitters, Dr Marshall spoke about a cure for cancer among other medical and spiritual topics. Leo said that no relatives of his came through, which was a pity as that would have provided that extra level of detailed evidence. Flint would bring through not only famous people's voices but also those of 'ordinary' men and women and many of the living relatives attending his seances were able to communicate directly with their loved ones in the most intimate ways.

Dr Dinshaw Nanji was a professor in the department of biology at Birmingham University, when sadly his wife Annie passed away from cancer in 1966. Dr Nanji became a regular visitor to the Flint seances from 1970 and spoke over a ten-year period to his late wife. Over that decade, she gave many clear and intimate messages, such as reminding him of his walk the previous day, where he had seen a lady down the street who had reminded him of Annie. He would confirm that he did indeed see an Annie lookalike in the street. She would mention his old, tattered hat, which he never wore to the seance but only out on walks. These were a few small but vital pieces of evidence that Flint could not have known.

A MURDERED POLICEMAN

Leslie Flint held his seances in his own home and in many other locations in different countries, often on stage in front of hundreds of people. At one event on Saturday, 14 February 1948, as witnessed by Alan Ernest Crossley and recounted in his book *A Journey of Psychic Discovery*, Flint was seated in a sealed cabinet in Kingsway Hall, central London, and the demonstration was chaired by Reverend Charles Drayton Thomas, as mentioned earlier.

A sound engineer, whose job it was to make sure that spirit voice box could be heard by the audience in the large hall, put some microphones just inside the seance cabinet and set their level so that Flint's own voice would be clearly audible through speakers placed around the hall. Strangely, although the audience could barely hear Flint, when his spirit guide Mickey came through his voice was booming and heard by all. The engineer even wrote out an affidavit to testify the voices had behaved in this way. At this same event a policeman who had very recently been murdered came through asking for his sister, who was in the audience. The late PC Edgar went on to say, 'The man they are looking for is in a boarding house, the gun is hidden under the mattress in his room.'

ANCIENT LANGUAGES

Flint was often accused of making the voices up and being a clever ventriloquist. At the same time, though, he was also one of the most tested mediums in the UK. Reports claim that he was required to drink coloured water and hold it in his mouth during a seance, while also having his mouth taped up. From 1967 to 1972 test seances with Flint were held by electrotechnical engineer Nigel Buckmaster, together with Prof William Bennet from Columbia University, USA. According to Buckmaster:

> 'His face [Flint's] was taped. His lips were sealed with plaster right across his face. And a microphone was put on his throat. A throat microphone. Again, of course, one never gets it absolutely cut and dry, but the fact that there were voices when his mouth was taped, and the voice produced perfect sounds of p's and b's, indicated to us that they were supernormal.... We did see in infrared light ectoplasm proceeding out of his left ear just above his shoulder and then on his shoulder. Professor Bennet and I were invited by Micky [Flint's guide] to come up close to it. We were not allowed to touch it. It looked like a very strange substance. I don't what it was, but it did build up, and the voice seemed to proceed from it.'

In the early 1970s, the Dutch ventriloquist Haak van Overloop (at the time, he was known as the best in the business) was asked to have his mouth plastered and then produce something intelligible for a test for a Dutch radio documentary on Flint. The only sound he could produce was 'mmmmmmmmmmmm'. Van Overloop said that for any ventriloquist it was absolutely impossible to produce p's and b's in such a situation (with a plaster stuck over one's mouth). So the claims made that Flint was a very good ventriloquist were by that point considered nonsense.

Yet still the voices would come through and sometimes, they would be heard speaking a foreign tongue that Flint could not possibly have known. Of course, the opposing point could be made that somehow Flint had learned Latin and was throwing his voice. How likely is it, though, that a medium in the Western world would have known ancient and even forgotten languages, which would involve years of intensive study?

Another medium who claimed to produce the voices of ancient spirits in their own language was named George Valiantine. He was tested by Dr Neville Whymant, a British professor of linguistics who was invited in 1921 to a series of seances in New York. Dr Whymant spoke 30 languages himself, so was well placed to detect any forgery. This medium used a seance trumpet to help amplify the weak voices coming through. Whymant, who was highly sceptical of such things, only agreed to attend because he knew and trusted the host of the seance, a respected judge and lawyer, William Cannon. George Valiantine, it was reported, was able to bring at least 14 languages through the metal seance trumpet, including Portuguese, Italian, Basque, Welsh, Japanese, Spanish, Russian, Hindustani and Chinese. New York was the arrival point for many immigrants and therefore had a mixed population. It was reported that many deceased friends and relatives spoke to sitters in their shared home language, and in recognizable voices, discussing matters Valiantine could not possibly have known about or researched.

For instance, on 25 February 1925, Madame Wellington Koo, who was at the time the first lady of China, was one of seven sitters with Valiantine. The countess later explained to author and researcher Herbert Bradley that the 'voice' that came through and spoke to her was with two Chinese dialects mixed together, in a way in which no European – even if he were able to speak Chinese – was able to do. She further explained, one of the dialects was that which her father, who had died the previous year, spoke to her when she was a young child, while the second dialect was one he used after she became an adult. The message was to be passed on by her to her own mother and therefore too personal for her to reveal to Bradley.

Whymant claimed that the trumpet rose off the floor and floated towards him. First, he heard the faint voice of his deceased father-in-law speaking to him in his distinctive English west country accent. Whymant was convinced no one in the seance room in New York would have ever known about his father-in-law. Then another voice spoke to him in an ancient Chinese language that was effectively a dead language and, like Latin or Sanskrit, no longer spoken colloquially. He understood what was being said to him but could only respond in a more modern version of Chinese. 'If this was a hoax, it was a particularly clever one, far beyond the scope of any of the sinologues [students of Chinese language and culture] now living,' Whymant said. The voice said, 'My mean name is K'ung, men call me Fu-tsu, and my lowly style is Kiu.' Whymant asked for the voice to repeat the name. This time without any hesitation at all came the name 'K'ung-fu-tzu,' Whymant wrote. This was the English spelling of the name we know today as Confucius, the 6th-century BCE Chinese philosopher.

CONVERSING WITH CONFUCIUS

Whymant continued, 'Now I thought, was my opportunity. Chinese I had long regarded as my own special research area, and he would be a wise man, medium or other, who would attempt to trick me on such soil. If this tremulous voice were that of the old ethicist who had personally edited the Chinese classics, then I had an abundance of questions to ask him. Then it burst upon me that I was listening to Chinese of a purity and delicacy not now spoken in any part of China.' The spirit voice apparently recognized that Whymant was finding it difficult to understand the ancient dialect, and changed to a more modern dialect.

Whymant decided he would test the spirit voice and remembered that there are several poems in Confucius' *Shih King* that baffled both Chinese and Western scholars. Whymant spoke to the voice in modern Chinese, 'This stupid one would know the correct reading of the verse in *Shih King*. It has been hidden from understanding for long centuries, and men look upon it with eyes that are blind. The passage begins thus, "Ts'ai ts'ai chüan êrh..."' Whymant recalled the first line of the third ode in the first book of Chou nan (the first book of the *Shih King*) although he could not remember the remaining 14 lines. In his book, Whyman wrote, 'The "voice" took up the poem and recited it to the end.' This voice also put a new construction on the verses so that it made sense to Whymant.

Whymant decided to give the spirit voice another test by asking the following. 'In *Lun Yü, Hsia Pien*, there is a passage that is wrongly written.

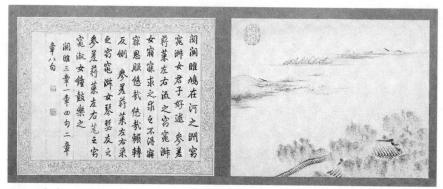

A sample from a Qing-dynasty era of the Shih King, *also known as* The Classic of Poetry. *First written more than 2,500 years ago, it contained several obscure passages – yet Valiantine's channelling of Confucius appeared to solve one of its mysteries.*

[These writings form part of Confucius' *Analects*, recounting events from his life.] Should it not read thus?' The voice interrupted Whymant before he could finish the question and continued the passage to the end, explaining that the copyists were in error, as the character written as 'sê' should have been 'i' and the character written as 'yen' was an error for 'fou'. This would no doubt have confused the other sitters at the seance, but it made perfect sense to Whymant. A literary mystery that had foxed scholars had apparently been solved by Confucius himself!

Whymant would go on to attend George Valiantine's seances 11 more times, and because of his linguistic skills he conversed with more spirits who spoke in a variety of languages. He said, 'They included Chinese, Hindi, Persian, Basque, Sanskrit, Arabic, Portuguese, Italian, Yiddish, (spoken with great fluency when a Yiddish- and Hebrew-speaking Jew was a member of the circle), German and modern Greek.' During one demonstration Whymant noticed Valiantine speaking American English to a sitter while at the same time a voice came through the trumpet speaking in a foreign tongue. This alone convinced him that Valiantine could not be directly throwing his voice, as some sceptics had claimed.

This is a truly fascinating account because opportunities to interrogate purported spirits from a position of expert knowledge is so rare. More often, it will be some type of technology that is used to build evidence, whether its aim is to prove or disprove an experience like direct voice mediumship as paranormal. In many cases it is those who claim to have psychic abilities themselves who actually deploy modern technology in an attempt to understand more.

SIR WINSTON CHURCHILL ON TRIAL

Leo Bonomo, the clairvoyant medium and psychical researcher who witnessed Leslie Flint materializing spirit voices using ectoplasm, commissioned a company called Primeau Forensics in 2018 to perform a spectral waveform analysis on the recording of a spirit voice purported to be that of Sir Winston Churchill that was heard at one of Flint's earlier seances. By providing the technicians in the US with a copy of an old recording done at the Flint seance, they were able to compare the waveforms of the Flint recordings against known recordings of Churchill, comparing speech patterns and peaks and troughs in the waveform to see similar matches, suggesting it is the same person in both recordings.

The company later reported a match between the voice claiming to be Sir Winston Churchill and actual recordings of Churchill with a confidence level over 99 per cent. In his book, *The Voice of Spirit*, Leo reported, 'This to me suggests Primeau Forensics have indicated a strong case of the existence of life after death. What is so special about this is that "the recording" was made 22 years after Sir Winston's death!' An interesting side note is that many of the spirits who came through Flint often complained about the etheric 'thought mask' that they were required to impress their thoughts into. Some of them did not like using it and perhaps felt a form of claustrophobia while using it. The mask is invisible to those on the Earth side of life, but very visible to those in the spirit world, just as they are invisible mostly to us.

A more recent example of direct voice and physical mediumship from 2008 involves the English-born physical medium David Thompson, who is based in Australia. A recording is heard of a husband who passed away attempting to use direct voice communication with his wife. He reports at the beginning how strange the process is for him and that he felt so nervous at the prospect of using such a method he was reluctant to carry on using it. He did persevere, however, after he was given further encouragement by the sitters. At the end of the seance, the husband managed to briefly materialize and then stroke and hug his wife slightly before vanishing and, as his voice leaves, the sound of air being sucked from the room is audible on the recording.

Some people report that David Thompson's seances are entirely genuine experiences, but he has also been criticized by others who have raised serious questions about his abilities. I understand that spirits of famous people including Louis Armstrong and Quentin Crisp (whose voices 'appeared' at another medium's demonstration discussed earlier in this book, which in my view was suspect) come through and may sing and converse with those in attendance. For me, better evidence is found when deceased relatives and friends of sitters come through via a medium and present personal 'insider' information, which makes it preferable to chats and singalongs with stars of the past.

Sceptics have criticized the voices produced by Leslie Flint as nothing more than ventriloquism. They have also suggested that he may have had accomplices in the room helping to produce the voices. However, Flint has been reported to have done on-the-spot seances with just himself and one sitter, as with Professor William R. Bennett in his own apartment in New York in September 1970, where the still voices presented themselves.

ELECTRONIC VOICE PHENOMENA

Direct voice mediumship is a very rare psychic ability and most mediums and psychics cannot produce direct voice phenomena. Spirit voices are more likely to be heard as electronic voice phenomena or EVP for short, either intentionally or accidentally. This is where spirits somehow manifest their voices on to tape recordings, or more recently digital audio, and may be heard when this is played back.

In 1952, Roman Catholic monks Father Pellegrino Ernetti and Father Agostino Gemelli, a former physician, were recording Gregorian chants on their new tape recorder, when it broke down. Frustrated, Father Gemelli is said to have looked to the heavens and asked for his 'father' to help them – no doubt an appeal to God, his heavenly father. Later on, when they listened to their recording both monks were amazed to hear the voice of Fr Gemelli's paternal late father responding. He was recorded as saying, 'Zucchini [his father's nickname for him] it is I, it is clear ... do you not know it is I? Of course I shall help you. I'm always with you.'

When the monks carried out more experiments it was said that further messages were left on the tape by Fr Gemelli's father. The monks took the brave step of contacting Pope Pius XII (1876–1958), who listened to the recording and whose response was surprisingly very positive. The Holy Father said the voice heard was of scientific fact and was objectively recorded, without any known spiritualist mediums present. It represented, he said, a cornerstone to build people's faith in a hereafter. The Pope wrote back after listening to a copy of the recording in 1952:

> 'Dear Father Gemelli, you really need not worry about this. The existence of this voice is strictly a scientific fact and nothing to do with spiritism. The recorder is totally objective... it receives and records only sound waves from wherever they come. This experiment may perhaps become the cornerstone for a building of scientific studies which will strengthen people's faith in a hereafter.'

Further development occurred in 1959 when the Swedish painter and film producer Friedrich Jürgenson was attempting to record wild birdsong on his tape recorder. As well as birds singing, when he played back the tape he could hear his late mother, who was German, speaking in her native tongue; 'Friedrich, you are being watched. Friedel, my little Friedel, can you hear me?' He continued to have more success with

Father Agostino Gemelli (centre) feared the spiritual implications of hearing the voice of his father on the tapes and contacted the Pope for further advice.

many more voices on his recordings, so much so that he became known as the 'father of EVP' and went on to write very popular books on the subject, including *Voices from the Universe* and *Radio Contact with the Dead.*

In his book, *Voice Transmissions with the Deceased*, Friedrich Jürgenson gives further accounts of his experimental recordings with the dead. He played the tapes at an international press conference and, in 1967, Latvian psychologist Dr Konstantin Raudive read the reports with great scepticism. He later visited Jürgenson to learn his methods of recording the dead and decided to experiment on his own and soon devised experimental techniques. Like Jürgenson, Raudive also heard the voice of his own deceased mother, who called him by his boyhood name, saying 'Kostulit, this is your mother.' Just as Jürgenson had, he catalogued tens of thousands of voices, most of which were under strict laboratory conditions.

A PHONE CALL FROM THE OTHER SIDE

Initially a sceptic, by 1967 Raudive had begun his own experiments into the paranormal. Raudive went on to record several successful EVP recordings. In fact, in 1972 he was thoroughly tested in England by top audio engineers. English publisher, Colin Smythe, arranged for Raudive's research to be scientifically tested, aided by electro-acoustic experts from Pye Records, namely Ken Attwood and Ray Prickett and in the presence, among others, of Colin Smythe, Peter Bander, Sir Robert Mayer, David Stanley and Ronald Maxwell. Four reel-to-reel tape recorders made by Nagra were shielded from radio interference and were recording for 18 minutes under the supervision of the aforementioned experts. Peter Bander confirmed the 'instruments recordings were taking place although the listeners [monitoring the recording in real time through their headphones] could hear nothing. On rewinding and playing back the tapes over 200 voices, of which 27 were clearly understandable, were heard.'

A further set of experiments was held in the screened chamber at the laboratories of Belling and Lee, in Enfield, England. This setup involved shielding for radio frequencies designed to prevent the intrusion of stray electro-magnetic waves, such as radio broadcasts. Experts such as Peter Hale, the top British expert in electronic frequencies screening techniques, together with Ralph Lovelock, a physicist and electronics expert, conducted the second series of recordings. Again, clear EVP voices were recorded. In his report back to Colin Smythe, Peter Hale said: 'From the results we obtained last Friday, something is happening which I cannot explain in normal physical terms.'

After Raudive passed over in 1974 the American EVP researcher Mark Macey claimed to have received a telephone call from him, and that the two spoke over the phone for around ten minutes. He said he received the first of eight calls from him beginning in 1994, and in later years he managed to record them by setting up recording devices connected to his three phone lines. The first call was unexpected, so he had not yet set up any recording equipment. Expecting and hoping for more out-of-this-world communications, he installed recorders into every socket of his house. According to Macey, the phone would ring and he would pick it up as any normal person would do. The difference would be the deeper tones of Raudive announcing himself to Macey in his thick accent. Macey would then ask permission to record the call, to which Raudive would agree. Raudive would advise Macey on technical details of how to improve the reception for picking up spirit communications.

During this call, which Macey recorded, Raudive instructed the researcher about techniques he could try to make his EVP work more successful. Raudive was not alone during this phone call, with Macey reporting that they were joined by the spirit of a bishop who had been dead some 200 years. In the recording Raudive can be heard to say he was going to 'pass the device' over to the bishop so that he too could speak. A small crackle is audible and then another voice comes on the line. If this call is genuine it is, to put it bluntly, mind-blowing to think that the spirit world is somehow capable of dialling in to a landline telephone.

It is interesting that the late Dr Raudive spoke about a 'device' and not a phone or radio, which suggests the spirit world has made tools or devices for communication with our world rather than using, say, telepathy. Maybe this was the 'thought mask' that Leo Bonomo described as he watched Leslie Flint materialize spirit voices in 1990. Whether or not that is the case, such gadgets somehow amplify either their voices or thoughts and turn them into signals that can somehow interact with our telephone systems. This is definitely not the only example of the paranormal world and human technology interacting to create a spirit, rather than a ghost, in the machine.

SPIRICOM

If the soul, or essence of a person really does continue on after the body dies, then it seems reasonable to think that people who were innovators in life will continue to develop and teach their knowledge and skills after they have passed into the spirit world. American psychical researchers George and Jeanette Meek were dedicated in their attempts to capture afterlife voices. In the 1970s and 1980s, with the help of medium William

O'Neil, they recorded hundreds of hours of EVP using radio transducers. These were essentially a form of interface, or adapter, that enabled two-way communications between Earth and the spirit world. They were allegedly able to capture conversations with the spirit of Dr George Jeffries Mueller, a university physics professor who passed away in 1967.

The system, known as Spiricom, enabled O'Neil a long two-way conversation with Mueller. He wanted to help O'Neil and the Spiricom team to develop their communication technology. Mueller managed to partly materialize in O'Neil's house in 1977 and speak to him about developing the Spiricom device.

Dr Mueller provided personal details of his former Earth life to O'Neil, to show him he was a bona fide person but just not inhabiting his earthly body anymore. He provided O'Neil with his social security number, gave the place where a copy of his death certificate could be found, complete details of his work at the University of Wisconsin and at Cornell University, as well as details on the various positions he had held in government and industry. Meek checked these details and located Mueller's former wife, who was able to verify much of what he had heard. Everything matched up.

It was O'Neil's electronics know-how and his unique ability as a medium that enabled the Spiricom to be developed. The actual device was a set of tone and frequency generators that emitted 13 tones spanning the range of the adult male voice. By the autumn of 1980, the Spiricom communications device had advanced to the point where Mueller's spirit voice was loud and easily understandable, despite the electronic modulation underlying it. Meek and O'Neil soon catalogued more than 20 hours of dialogue with their spirit colleague Mueller, reported in some detail in Meek's book *After We Die, What Then?*

Mueller himself remarked he did sound like a robot coming through. Listening to YouTube recordings of these amazing sessions, you can indeed compare the voice coming through to that of the feared Cylon robots from the original 1980s series of science fiction television series *Battlestar Galactica*. Perhaps the modulation of those voices were done in a similar way to deliberately produce distortions for the TV show, whereas O'Neil was doing his best to clear up the robotic sounds. However, just trying to clear that up could risk losing the connections required.

Critics frequently claimed that O'Neil was always around during the recordings and was in fact a ventriloquist. However, for these types of communications to work a medium or sensitive must be present to help channel or focus the spirit energy. Even if the device appears to be plugged in to the mains for electrical power, the voices only seem to work in the presence of a medium. If the medium walks away, then the voices cease to be.

Spiricom had its fair share of detractors, and some suggested that O'Neil was a ventriloquist. After he passed away, a device known as an Electrolarynx was found in his house. It is possible that this was the cause of the electronic sounds that came with the spirit voice. This device is usually used by people who have lost their voice, and picks up vibrations from the user's throat and amplifies them to allow their speech to be heard. Other sceptical reports suggest that O'Neil suffered from schizophrenia.

The inventors of Spiricom went to some effort to write a manual on how to build it, but cautioned that you really needed a human medium to be part of the connection to make it all work. Without it, the machine would be like a radio without a power source. In their *Spiricom Tech Manual* they say: '*It also seems to use the auric energy field of one of our technicians [O'Neil] who is such an advanced psychic that his clairaudient and clairvoyant abilities have on occasion allowed him to converse with and see the dead person. His energies have, on at least one occasion, been utilized in a full body materialization of a spirit form. To date, our only extensive two-way conversations have been obtained when this technician is present in the room in which the equipment is located.*'

The actual device went through four different variations before they presented it to the world, and by the Mark 4 version, they had a high frequency RF generator, a foot-long antenna, a demodulator, a preamplifier, microphone, and a tape recorder. After presenting the invention at the National Press Club in Washington D.C. in 1982, to a less than receptive press audience, the invention fell into obscurity. Two years later, a senior electronics technician at the famed Massachusetts Institute of Technology, Erland Babcock, managed to obtain a grant to work on a similar machine.

ITALIAN SPIRIT RADIO

Rather than using recording technology to capture paranormal voices, Italian Marcello Bacci claimed to tune into transmissions from discarnate spirits using an old-fashioned shortwave valve radio. He used nothing more than an old wireless radio that somehow was picking up the intentional transmissions of discarnate spirits.

He became interested in the possibility of life after death after attending a mediumship demonstration in London in 1949. By the 1960s he was developing his radio communications using the direct radio voice method. This is more advanced than EVP, where the experimenter uses a tape recorder to record the silence of the room, asks questions aloud and then plays back the tape to see if a spirit has left an answering message. Tuning into the waveband of 7 to 9 MHz, voices would be heard sometimes for ten seconds and sometimes up to four minutes in duration. Many visitors supposedly recognized the voices as their deceased loved ones and in many cases, the dead children of villagers were said to speak out to their mothers eagerly waiting in Bacci's visitor centre in Tuscany. The voices were clear, similar to the audio you would hear on an old-style analogue radio.

Since 1974, scientist Paolo Pressi and his colleagues in El Laboratories, Italy have been investigating Bacci and his DRV or Direct Radio Voice phenomena. They have not yet found the slightest evidence of fraud. Paulo Pressi said of Bacci, 'the voices that are coming from out of his radio are very very astonishing because the content level is very high in respect of the culture of Mr Bacci because he was only a businessman *with a shop of washing machines and radios and so forth.'* In other words, respectively, Pressi is saying that Bacci is a simple uneducated man, but the voices presenting themselves out of his old wireless radio are very high in intelligence. The voices would vary according to who was coming through. Some would come through and say, *'Death is a transition, here we live in another dimension.'* Others would just say hello to their loved ones who might be present.

When some of the voices were analyzed by Pressi in the early 2000s using software similar to that used by the FBI, he found a 97 per cent match between the 'spirit' voice and the voice in video and audio cassette recordings made when that person was alive. In 2002 the technician Franco Santi removed two valves from the radio responsible for receiving normal AM and FM broadcasts. Even without the valves, the voices continued to pour from the speakers. In another experiment in 2003, Dr Carlos Trajina, an engineer, set up a second radio beside Bacci's old wireless and tuned it to the same short-wave frequencies. However, Bacci's wireless was the only one that continued to receive the transmissions from the afterlife.

Trajina then put the radio inside a radio signal proof casing to ensure Bacci was not transmitting the signals from another location. Still the voices broke through. Santi was attempting to understand the origin of the transmission as well as root out whether Marcello could be a hoax. After examining his radios, he found nothing out that could explain the mysterious reception and sources of the broadcasts.

Without Marcello Bacci present, the radios never picked up anything but normal transmissions. Was this evidence that Marcello was a fraud, using sleight of hand to trick everyone, or could it be that Marcello had mediumistic abilities and acted as a conduit through which the spirits could reach back into our world? Details of Bacci's work can be viewed in the documentary *Calling Earth*.

Even more astounding, it was reported that when the old wireless device was unplugged from the mains, which would stop it working, the discarnate voices could still be heard. If these reports are genuine, it suggests that the success of EVP depends in very large part on the abilities of each medium, who seems to act as the 'channel' or consciousness that these communications pass through.

Some have suggested that Bacci's version of EVP was little more than random snippets of live radio broadcasts as he tuned in the radio for lengthy periods, together with a few pre-recorded phrases. Supposedly, though, the voices were recognized by the independent sitters in the room, and gave out specific personal family information. They were reported to have spoken in the local Italian dialect of that region, which would rule out nationally broadcast transmissions.

Even more compelling, when members of the famous Scole psychic experiment group in England visited Bacci in 2004 to witness a demonstration, the voices coming through Bacci's radio speakers reportedly changed from the Italian dialect to English and addressed the Scole team specifically. Apparently the Italian 'team' of spirits had moved aside to allow the Scole 'team' to communicate. These elements were confirmed by Professor Mario Salvatore Festa, Professor of Physics at the University of Naples, who also put his ear to the speaker after the radio valves were removed and the power switched off, to confirm that voices were still coming from it.

THE SCOLE EXPERIMENT

The Scole Experiment occurred in the early 1990s in the village of Scole in Norfolk, England. A group consisting of psychic researchers and mediums worked together to try to establish communication with the afterlife. These experiments were known for generating various phenomena, including extra-terrestrials whose images were imposed on photographs. It's interesting to note that supposedly the great Thomas Edison himself transmitted instructions from the afterlife to the Scole team on how to improve radio communications between earth and the hereafter. He did so in the unique method for which Scole is so well known. During their basement seance experiments, the five psychic researchers placed a brand new 35 mm slide or transparency film on a table in the darkened room.

When the film was processed in what was then the normal way and then returned, the researchers were stunned to see the whole film had writing across it and pictures, in a kind of Bayeux Tapestry effect, as well as instructions on how to add extra devices to the electronic equipment to improve their spirit communications. The instructions were signed in the same way that Edison used to sign his letters when living, suggesting the famous inventor was continuing to try and push boundaries, by reaching out to help remove the barriers between this world and the next. While we don't know that Edison's advice was ever acted on, other refinements in communication technology have come along, while others are looking at exciting new inventions.

Robin Foy, one of the original Scole team participants, has gone on record stating as well as getting photographs of aliens on camera, they also came into contact with an ET called Varane. Robin described this alien as a lord of the cosmos who got in touch with them right at the end of their last four sittings to explain why they would have to close down the Scole group. Varane described another psychic research group similar to the Scole group that existed in a future time period. Unfortunately for the Scole team, it was interfering with their own group sittings and prevented them from working correctly. Robin said that noises like 'screams' could be heard coming through their crystals that they had laid out on their small table. These 'screams' stopped the two Scole mediums, Alan and Diana Bennett, from going into their regular trances. The screaming sounds were not people in pain or suffering but merely a side effect from the group of the future.

After the Scole Experiment closed in 1998, Robin Foy and his wife Sandra moved to Spain, where he continued his research into life after death until his own passing in 2018. Professor Arthur Ellison, Professor David Fontana and historian Montague Keen, along with members of the Society of Psychical Research, chronicled their Scole investigations in

The Scole Report between 1995 and 1997. All three main investigators concluded that something 'interesting to science' had occurred during the Scole Experiment. Alan and Diana Bennett were inspired to do further studies in the field of the paranormal and went on to form a second group called the Norfolk Experimental Group with authors Jane and Grant Solomon, which ran from 2005 to 2007. In the later trials, they conducted their experiments in the daylight, focusing light beams on to crystals on reflective surfaces and photographing the results, which they claimed were faces, objects and buildings.

GHOST BOX

The 'ghost box' or spirit box is still basically a radio, but also a modern version of Bacci's device because it is modified to more easily tune into the spirit world. It continually scans different radio frequencies, skipping around to find spirit voices or other paranormal audio within the white noise. Ghost boxes are portable and commercially available devices that can also be used to record audio. They tend to get better results when operated by real mediums, as if the medium is a signal-boosting aerial and the box is the amplified result of this signal going through the aerial.

Philip Kinsella, the medium mentioned earlier, has reported significant results using a ghost box device. In 2010, one of the first communications he received came through from a young man who'd been killed in a car accident. Philip asked him some basic questions like his name and the male voice came back instantly with the name Michael. The voice began to waver in and out of signal, before fading out. Philip left the ghost box on 'sweep' mode for the next hour and he was stunned when Michael returned and called out his name from the ghost box!

Michael gave brief details of who he was and Philip and his group of researchers considered the possibility of reaching out to Michael's mother with the information they had received from him. But they decided to wait in case it was taken the wrong way. Philip, as the medium, acted as a connecting power to help bring in the spirit voices to the ghost box, in the same way Bacci in Italy had attracted the spirit voices to his old wireless. Philip's team of fellow researchers, like an audience at a seance, provided additional energy to help manifest the connection.

SCIENTISTS AND A SOLDIER SON

On another occasion Philip called out the name of a well-known scientist who had died and he promptly turned up, bringing another scientist with him. Philip had been asking about the Large Hadron Collider, the huge particle accelerator located near Geneva. He wanted to know if the Collider had a hidden purpose, possibly connected with opening portals to other dimensions. Suddenly, Philip heard warm laughter emanating through the ghost box from one of the scientists, as if he was jokingly saying, 'Ah, now then, we can't give you that information!' During a more advanced communication, Philip and his development circle of other mediums came across some British soldiers who had been killed in the war in Iraq. From his book, *Guardians of the Dead*, Philip recounts the episode.

'We had all been amazed when the voice of a male came through the ghost box. He gave his name as Stuart and it turned out that he'd been killed, along with his men, in Iraq. I recall most vividly that the session had one of the mediums present in tears because she couldn't believe this guy was communicating so well from his side of life. He gave some personal details about where he lived, that he missed his mum and that he and his men were ok now that they'd crossed over. The soldiers recall being shot and murdered in cold blood with their bodies being kicked. One lady in the group named Sue was a psychic artist and asked Stuart whether he would like her to compose his portrait. You can imagine the shock from everyone present when Stuart replied: 'Yes, like the Queen.' A large portrait of Her Majesty hung on the wall directly above us and everyone, including myself, gasped at this amusing gesture from the

A section of the Large Hadron Collider. Philip Kinsella theorized that it may have a secret role of opening portals to other dimensions.

soldier. I dared pose a question to Stuart. Although I knew the answer, I needed him to clarify something for me. 'Is the other side as beautiful as they say it is?' I'd asked. His reply came back almost instantly: 'Much more!'

The following week, Sue had finished Stuart's portrait and he came through the box once more to tell the circle of mediums how much he liked it. The group discussed whether they should contact Stuart's mother and maybe set up the ghost box so she could hear Stuart speaking through it for herself, but decided that it was too early to be confident enough to guarantee its performance should they set it up in his mother's home. Once a more widely understood and publicly available communication technology, like a phone, becomes available there will be less concern about, for example, people pretending to be mediums targeting vulnerable people and telling them only they can help them contact a loved one who has passed over.

THE SOUL PHONE PROJECT

This project at the University of Arizona's Laboratory for Advances in Consciousness and Health is currently in the prototype phase of various types of device to make contact with what the team calls 'postmaterial persons' (PMPs). Long term, the project aims to develop technology that isn't in any way reliant on a medium's abilities. At present the most developed and tested prototype is the Soul Switch, a simple switching device that blinks a light on for 'yes' and off for 'no' that can be operated by PMPs in order to answer questions. The project team, including mediums, software developers and electrical engineers, has claimed that since 2019 it has been achieving what it calls 'rudimentary communication' with spirits using the switch device. Other variations include an audio device that would allow the spirit's voice to come through and speak in real time with living beings. This will be a slow process, according to team leader Gary E. Schwartz PhD, because modern electromagnetic 'noise' like Wi-fi signals means the spirit signal at present is like an inch-tall person trying to be heard among giants, although he added that improvements have been made.

Even more intriguing is the project's attempt to involve 'postmaterial luminaries' in further developing these prototypes. It namechecks Edison, Marconi and Alexander Graham Bell as individuals who were all keen to develop a means of communicating with the afterlife, so could these scientific greats be reaching to today's innovators to help them develop direct communication links between worlds? Elsewhere, there are also unconfirmed reports from different sources that Steve Jobs, the late Apple Computers founder, is one such mind who has already communicated with mediums on this side and is keen to help develop Earth technology to reach through to the other side.

Medium Stephanie Patel, a retired lawyer, claims she is in contact with the late Apple Computers founder on a telepathic basis. While he chats with her, he is also kept busy with another project with some pretty high brow names associated with it. The Apple computers founder has been named by Dr Gary E. Schwartz of the Soul Phone Foundation as one of the teams on the other side of the veil as helping in the development of technology to bridge the gap between the worlds.

In a press release issued by Schwartz in 2017, he named other spirit collaborators including theoretical physicists Albert Einstein, who developed the theory of relativity, and Max Planck and David Bohm, both quantum physicists.

Additionally listed in the afterlife development team are the inventor of the phonograph, Thomas Edison, electrical engineer and famed inventor Nikola Tesla, the mathematician James Clerk Maxwell, and famous TV astronomer Carl Sagan. Along with the scientists, the other world team includes the magician and escapologist Harry Houdini, who investigated claims of spiritualism when he was alive on this side, his friend, author and spiritualist Sir Arthur Conan Doyle, the creator of Sherlock Holmes.

THE CHRISTIAN CHURCH AND THE AFTERLIFE

While modern technology heads towards direct connection between the living and dead (or passed-over or PMPs, if you prefer), communicating with the deceased is one of the key points of difference between spiritualism and organized Christian religion. While some spiritualists believe in a divine being or intelligence, they do not think we are judged at death, but instead that our essence or soul continues, just as it was when we were in our physical body, moving to a dimension where it continues to evolve and learn. And this means, therefore, that we can connect directly with those who are in the spirit world via a medium. The Old and New Testaments both contain verses that are vehemently against this. One example, Leviticus 20, includes the warning, 'I will set my face against anyone who turns to mediums and spiritists'.

The Christian faith asserts that upon death you are met by Jesus. If you accepted him as your saviour when on Earth, he forgives you of your sins and welcomes you to a heavenly abode. It's through God's forgiveness of our sins that the dead can go on to heaven to continue their lives. Only by accepting Jesus as the saviour, who takes on the sins of the world are you given a fresh start and absolved of any wrongdoing.

The residents of the spiritualistic version of the afterlife have a different approach. Certainly, the accounts given by Monsignor Hugh Benson, who died in 1914, and returned through the mediumship of Anthony Borgia, if they are to be believed, tell a very different story. He said in the book *Life in the Unseen World*, published in 1954, that he was ill on his death bed and felt a sudden urge to rise up. He followed through with this inner urge and sat upright on his bed, and suddenly came face to face with his late friend Edwin who had died many years before him. Benson knew immediately he had died and felt comforted that Edwin had come to meet him. In the book, he describes how he moved on into the spirit world with Edwin as his guide and friend. There was no judgement by God or Jesus, and Benson said that one judged oneself in the afterlife. There was no Hell or eternal Damnation, but there was something called the lower realms. This was an area of the spirit world he said where those less evolved souls would eventually wind up. They were not left there and many higher spirits would go there to try and uplift them out of their own self-made misery. Jesus was mentioned very little in the book and its succeeding volumes.

THE CHURCH OF ENGLAND INVESTIGATES

In the late 1930s the Church of England, under Archbishop of Canterbury William Cosmo Gordon Lang, commissioned a report into spiritualism and communication with the afterlife. Nine of the 12 authors of the report came out in favour of spiritualism and its benefit to the bereaved. They concluded by saying, 'When every possible explanation of these [spirit] communications has been given, and all doubtful evidence set aside, it is generally agreed that there remains some element as yet unexplained. We think that it is probable that the hypothesis that they proceed in some cases from discarnate spirits is a true one.'

However, this report was suppressed by the archbishop, who was 'disappointed' by the conclusions. It contrasted too much with the Church's teachings of being judged and sent to Hell if you were not worthy. Those spirits communicating through mediums were describing an afterlife in which everyone who was in spirit went to the same place, a spirit world. There was no mention of Heaven, Hell, judgement or eternal punishment. Every spirit had the opportunity to reach towards perfection, from whatever state or 'sphere' they came from. Spiritualism was an attractive alternative for many people, which may have been a source of anxiety within the Church.

THE ARCHBISHOP SPEAKS?

The suppressed report finally saw the light of day when it was secretly delivered to the offices of the *Psychic News* newspaper in the 1947, possibly by a sympathetic supporter within the Church of England, making world headlines. A full account appeared in 1979 in the journal of the *Churches' Fellowship for Psychic and Spiritual Studies* (CFPSS). Many Christians, including many of those working within the Church of England, appear to be unaware of its existence. Today a branch of spiritualism exists called Christian Spiritualism, whose members believe there is a spirit world beyond our physical existence and spirits work in this plane as guides, and also that Jesus' teachings should be followed to help others and in doing so become closer to God. Although Dr Lang suppressed the report he may himself have had second thoughts; he was reported to have returned in spirit through the direct voice mediumship of Leslie Flint! A purported recording of the archbishop's spirit voice from 1 October 1960 said:

'I say to you, there is only one way in which the world can be saved from itself, and that is by the realisation that love over cometh all things, and that those who have gone before you are concerned for you, each one. And we come back to your world, endeavoring to break down the barriers that you have created, by foolishness and ignorance over the centuries, and we knock at your door hoping and praying that you will open it just a little, that we may enter therin and save you from yourselves.' (Courtesy of The Leslie Flint Trust).

Conan Shaw, a well-known psychical researcher who knew Dr Lang listened to the tape and wrote, 'After hearing and studying this tape I should like to place the following on record: As a chorister in York Minster (1908–15) I had many opportunities of coming into direct contact with Dr Lang. On a number of special occasions I was chosen to carry the archbishop's train. His slow style of speech comes out well on the tape as do his mannerisms. Both hands would clasp the top of his stole, then he would build up to a climax on one word or one phrase as he does on the tape to the word "now" and the phrase "then they shall stand up in the church and proclaim it" [this refers to spiritualistic communication]. His head would turn left to right, then right to left and centre, observantly getting his three points home to the whole congregation. Yes, I have every confidence it is Dr Cosmo Lang who is the communicator as he claims to be on the tape.'

If this was in fact the spirit of the former Archbishop of Canterbury, there is a certain irony to his return through mediumship to spread a message of love and open-mindedness. However, as we saw with the Catholic monk whose father spoke to him through a tape recorder, he would not be the first person with a deep Christian faith who claimed to have received messages directly from the afterlife. Next we will turn our attention away from religion and towards the scientific world, and its approach to the paranormal, meeting those few who, it could be said, were brave enough to take Dr Lang's advice to break down barriers.

Former Archbishop of Canterbury, William Cosmo Gordon Lang.

CHAPTER SEVEN

SCIENCE INVESTIGATES THE PARANORMAL

'It argues ill for the boasted freedom of opinion among scientific men that they have so long refused to institute a scientific investigation into the existence and nature of facts asserted by so many competent and credible witnesses….For my own part, I too much value the pursuit of truth, and the discovery of any new fact in Nature, to avoid inquiry because it appears to clash with prevailing opinions.' So said Sir William Crookes, the first truly eminent British scientist to engage in serious research into psychic phenomena. However, while he believed scientists had a duty to investigate, his scientific contemporaries' response to the increasing public interest in spiritualism and the afterlife ranged from hostile to indifferent. In this chapter we will look at some of those early developments in thinking around the possible existence of dimensions other than ours, and the brave individuals who went against 'prevailing opinions' to put the paranormal under a microscope. The first strange tale involves two young sisters who, as we might say today, made the afterlife go viral.

SIR WILLIAM CROOKES AND KATE FOX

Sir William Crookes (1832–1919) was a highly influential and success-ful British chemist and physicist who attended the Royal College of Chemistry in London. His particular focus was on spectroscopy, the interaction between matter and electromagnetic radiation, and through this he discovered the magnetic element called thallium, a heavy metal used today in the manufacture of electronic components, optical lenses, semiconductor materials, and even artists' paints. His work is credited with laying the foundations for atomic physics: the invention in 1875 of the Crookes tube, a sealed glass container capable of carrying electricity, paved the way for the discovery of the X-ray and the electron. He even developed polarizing lenses used in modern sunglasses! Professor Crookes' impeccable scientific credentials were recognized with numerous honours including fellowship of the Royal Society and his knighthood in 1897.

His scientific investigations of the world of psychic phenomena arose from the personal loss of his younger brother Philip, which led him to investigate the claims of spiritualists. His stance at the beginning of his investigations was that he believed the whole thing to be a trick upon the public. Much of the scientific world of Victorian London, where there was no shortage of fraudsters, was in agreement (a fact noted by Sir Arthur Conan Doyle in his history of the subject). Crookes began to attend seances and mediumship demonstrations, and came to believe that this was an area with some genuine phenomena that deserved further scientific exploration.

Between 1871 and 1874 he took the opportunity to examine and test the American medium Kate Fox, one of the famous Fox sisters,

Sir William Crookes had a genuine interest in making scientific investigations into the paranormal.

whose strange childhood experiences in the mid-19th century, known as the 'Hydesville rappings', helped to establish the public interest in spiritualism and the afterlife.

THE HYDESVILLE RAPPINGS

In March 1848, Margaret and Kate Fox, then aged nine and 14, claimed to have made contact with a spirit in their home in Hydesville, New York. They communicated with the spirit they called 'Mr Splitfoot', who they said rapped on the walls and furniture in their house. These raps were basic responses to questions posed by the sisters: one rap for yes, two for no and so on. Through the long process of answering the questions, the raps indicated that in life the spirit had been a peddler (or travelling salesman) called Charles B. Rosna, who claimed he had been murdered at the house some years before and buried in the cellar. The sisters' claims soon gained widespread attention and they began to hold public demonstrations where they would communicate with spirits through raps and other means. This caused a sensation and Margaret and Kate became famous throughout the US and Europe. They were instrumental in spiritualism's rapid development into a popular movement, as many people sought to communicate with their deceased loved ones.

THE SCIENTIST'S EVALUATION

After his time with Miss Fox, William Crookes wrote, 'For power and certainty I have met with no one who at all approached Miss Kate Fox. For several months I enjoyed almost unlimited opportunity of testing the various phenomena occurring in the presence of this lady, and I especially examined the phenomena of these sounds. With mediums generally it is necessary to sit for a formal seance before anything is heard; but in the case of Miss Fox it seems only necessary for her to place her hand on any substance for loud thuds to be heard in it, like a triple pulsation, sometimes loud enough to be heard several rooms off. In this manner I have heard them in a living tree, on a sheet of glass, on a stretched iron wire, on a stretched membrane, a tambourine, on the roof of a cab and on the floor of a theatre. Moreover, actual contact is not always necessary; I have had these sounds proceeding from the floor, walls, etc., when the medium's hands and feet were held, when she was standing on a chair, when she was suspended in a swing from the ceiling, when she was enclosed in a wire cage, when she had fallen fainting on a sofa. With a full knowledge of the numerous theories which have been started, chiefly in America, to explain these sounds, I have tested them in every way that I could devise, until there has been no escape from the conviction that they were true objective occurrences not produced by trickery or mechanical means.'

Professor Crookes continued: 'I have observed many circumstances which appear to show that the will and intelligence of the medium have much to do with the phenomena... I have observed some circumstances which seem conclusively to point to the agency of an outside intelligence not belonging to any human being in the room.' In his examination of Fox he observed the movement of objects at a distance and the production of percussive sounds or raps. The latter raps covered a great range of sound, 'delicate ticks, detonations in the air, sharp metallic taps, a crackling like that heard when a frictional machine is at work, sounds like scratching, the twittering as of a bird, etc.' Crookes wondered about the extent to which the medium controlled them. The medium could be in one corner of the room, while sounds and objects out of sight would be heard or moved beyond any ability of the medium to physically produce the movement or sound.

A CONFESSION OF FRAUD?

Professor Crookes' credibility, and with it the existence of the spirit world, was called into question when in 1888, Margaret Fox, Kate's sister, confessed that the raps had been a hoax and that the sisters had produced the strange noises by cracking their toe joints. But was this really the truth? Many of Hydesville's local population said they also questioned the spirit of the peddler for confirmation of their own personal circumstances such as their ages, and personal family information. Could the young Fox sisters really have known such details?

Three investigative committees examined the Fox sisters in Rochester, New York between 1849 and 1850, with each committee being more rigorous and critical than the previous one. The rapping noises were loud enough to be clearly heard in a large hall before a crowded audience. The first committee reported that the sounds were heard on the wall, on the outside of a front door and on a closet door. It noted, 'By placing the hand upon the door, there was a sensible jar felt when the rapping was heard. One of the committee placed one of his hands upon the feet of the ladies and one on the floor, and though the feet were not moved, there was a distinct jar upon the floor.'

Some were sceptical of this first report and a new assessment committee was appointed, this time including a doctor, two town councillors and two assessors. This time, testing for knocks and raps was carried out in a lawyer's office, and Margaret Fox was the only sister present. According to this committee, sounds were heard in all directions including 'on the floor, chairs, table, walls, door, and, in fact, everywhere'.

The third examination was done this time by a 'committee of ladies' organized by the townsfolk of Hydesville, with the same raps again being heard. This time the committee took a different approach to testing. One member said, 'When they were standing on pillows, with a handkerchief tied to the ankles, we all heard the rapping on the wall and floor distinctly.' What is also interesting is that many of their questions that were mental or telepathic were correctly answered by the sisters.

What is less well-known is that raps were also reportedly heard by a previous tenant of the house, and that other local people claimed phenomena continued to occur after the Fox family had moved to a neighbouring house to escape the noises. Mr Duesler, a local man, said in evidence concerning his experiences, 'I then asked it to rap the number of years of my age. It rapped thirty times. This is my age, and I do not think anyone about here knew it, except myself and family. I then told it to rap my wife's age, and it rapped thirty times, which is her exact age; several of us counted it at the same time. I then continued to ask it to rap the ages of different persons – naming them – in the room, and it did so correctly, as they all said. I then asked the number of children in the different families in the neighbourhood, and it told them correctly in the usual way, by rapping; also the number of deaths that had taken place in the different families, and it told them correctly.'

The three Fox sisters, Margaret (left), Kate (centre) and Leah (right).

In my view, the initial rapping caused by the spirit of the peddler may have come about due to his inability to cross over to the other side because he had died by murder. The fact that he was able to communicate in raps before the Fox sisters moved into the house, and the sounds persisted after they were removed, suggests that he may have been able to use the power of its previous inhabitants and the joint energies of the visiting neighbours, similar to a poltergeist. However, the Fox sisters were probably natural mediums (those who did not need training to express their psychic talents) and thus able to produce rapping noises during the demonstrations they gave on their travels around the US and Britain. Perhaps the spirit of the murdered peddler travelled with them or they were producing manifestations of physical mediumship, that could have developed into spirit materializations given the right conditions for development.

Despite various committee assessments and positive receptions at demonstrations, some were not happy. This was especially true of the medical establishment. After witnessing a public demonstration in Buffalo, New York in 1851, they gave a full report to local newspapers at the time, telling everyone not to waste their money. Three physicians from the University of Buffalo, Austin Flint, Charles A. Lee, and C. B. Coventry, reported on their observations in a letter to the editor of the *Buffalo Commercial Advertiser* published on 17 February 1851.

'*Curiosity having led us to visit the room at the Phelps House in which two females from Rochester (Mrs. Fish and Miss Fox) profess to exhibit striking manifestations of the spiritual world, by means of which communion may be held with deceased friends, &c. and having arrived at a physiological explanation of the phenomena, the correctness of which has been demonstrated in an instance that has since fallen under observation, we have felt that a public statement is called for, which may perhaps serve to prevent further waste of time, money, and credulity (to say nothing of sentiment and philosophy) in connection with this so long successful imposition... it is taken for granted that the rappings are not produced by artificial contrivances about the persons of the females, which may be concealed by the dress. This hypothesis is excluded, because it is understood that the females have been repeatedly and carefully examined by lady committees. It is obvious that the rappings are not caused by machinery attached to tables, doors, etc., for they are heard in different rooms, and different parts of the same room, in which the females are present, but always near the spot where the females are stationed. This mechanical hypothesis is then to be excluded. So much for negative evidence, and now for what positively relates to the subject. On carefully observing the countenances of the two females, it was evident that the sounds were due to the agency of the younger sister, and that they involved an effort of the will. She evidently attempted to conceal any indications of voluntary effort, but in this she did not succeed:—a voluntary effort was manifest, and it was plain that it could not be continued very long without fatigue. Assuming, then, this positive fact, the inquiry arises, how can the will be exerted to produce sounds (rappings) without obvious movements of the body?*

The voluntary muscles are the only organs (save those which belong to the mind itself) over which volition can exert any direct control. But the contractions of the muscles do not, in the muscles themselves, occasion obvious sounds. The muscles, therefore, to develop audible vibrations, must act upon parts with which they are connected. Now, it was sufficiently clear that the rappings were not vocal sounds: these could not be produced without movements of the respiratory muscles, which would at once lead to detection. Hence, excluding vocal sounds, the only possible source of the noises in question, produced, as we have seen they must be, by voluntary muscular contractions, is in one or more of the movable articulations of the skeleton. From the anatomical connections of the voluntary muscles, this explanation remains as the only alternative. By an analysis prosecuted in this manner, we arrive at the conviction that the rappings, assuming that they are not spiritual, are produced, by the action of the will, through voluntary muscles, upon the joints.'

A BODY IN THE CELLAR

Some years later, there was a fascinating twist in the story of the Fox sisters and the Hydesville rappings. At the time of the initial rappings, the cellar where the peddler claimed to be buried could not be excavated fully due to flooding. In 1904 children playing in the house found something unsettling. On 23 November the *Boston Journal*, a non-spiritualist paper, reported, 'The skeleton of the man, supposed to have caused the rappings first heard by the Fox sisters in 1848, has been found in the walls of the house occupied by the sisters, and clears them from the only shadow of doubt held concerning their sincerity in the discovery of spirit communication. The Fox sisters declared they learned to communicate with the spirit of a man, and that he told them he had been murdered, and buried in the cellar. Repeated excavations failed to locate the body, and thus give proof positive of their story. William H. Hyde, a reputable citizen, who owns the house, made an investigation, and found an almost entire human skeleton between the earth and crumbling cellar walls, undoubtedly that of the wandering pedlar who, it was claimed, was murdered in the east room of the house, and whose body was hidden in the cellar along with the this pedlar's tin box discovered alongside it.'

Whatever the truth of the Fox sisters' experiences and their psychical abilities, they numbered some luminaries of technological advancement among their supporters. These included John Logie Baird, the Scottish electrical engineer and inventor of the television and Guglielmo Marconi, the Italian engineer and inventor of the wireless. It has been said that Baird developed television as an effort to communicate with the spirit world and Marconi, like Edison, later investigated the possibility of communicating with the spiritual dimension using his radio devices. Sir William Crookes, the eminent chemist and physicist, also continued his science-based investigations into the world beyond our own, with fascinating results, as recounted in the coming pages.

However, interest in the paranormal from the most rational, and most brilliant, minds was not new, even before the explosion of public curiosity in spiritualism witnessed in the 19th century and fuelled by the rapid development of entertainment and communication industries. One such genius was the Swedish polymath Emanuel Swedenborg (1688–1772), once described as 'the most extraordinary man in recorded history'.

EMANUEL SWEDENBORG AND 'CORRESPONDENCE'

Swedenborg was a visionary philosopher and theologian, in addition to his many scientific and mathematical accomplishments. He established Sweden's first scientific journal, *Daedalus Hyperboreus*, and published works on mathematics, cosmology and geology, among other subjects. At a relatively advanced age, having studied and written on the division between mind and body and the relationship of the soul to the physical being, he turned his attention to the paranormal.

According to Swedenborg, at this time the spiritual world had opened up to him and he was in contact with angels and devils in other dimensions. He published his first theological work, *Arcana Coelestia* (Secrets of Heaven) in 1749, and the eighth and final volume in 1756. *Secrets of Heaven* is a verse-by-verse breakdown of the inner spiritual meaning of the Bible, starting at the book of Genesis and moving through to Exodus. Swedenborg said that the Bible should not be taken literally but instead read as a spiritual guide. It should be interpreted with an inner spiritual meaning that was based on his concept of 'correspondence': that everything in our physical world is related to, and a reflection of, the spiritual world – for example, sunlight in our world corresponds to divine love in the spiritual world.

Swedenborg wrote further books on the subject such as *Heaven and Hell*, a description of the afterlife and the lives of its inhabitants, and *White Horse*, which explained more about the inner meaning of the Bible. In *Other Planets* he described the beings that live on other planets,

Emanuel Swedenborg, one of Sweden's leading Enlightenment philosophers and scientists, insisted that everything in our world has its own correspondence in the spiritual world.

some within our solar system and some living outside it in other star systems and galaxies. Swedenborg was a man far ahead of his time, and the rigour and clarity of his thought helped to build an understanding of the nature and possibilities of our world and the next a century before spiritualism as a movement came into the wider consciousness during the Victorian era.

SIR OLIVER LODGE

One eminent Victorian scientist who later in life would explore the idea of the existence of a spirit world and afterlife was Sir Oliver Lodge. Born in 1851 in Staffordshire, England, he was a British physicist involved in the development of patents for radio and also known for identifying electromagnetic radiation. Lodge also demonstrated an early radio wave detector he named the 'coherer', which allowed Morse code signals to be identified, enabling early wireless telegraph communication.

He initially had no interest in anything psychic or life after death, noting in the late 1870s, '*It did not seem to me possible that man could survive the death of the body. I did not think we could ever know the truth about things of that kind and was content with whatever destiny lay in store for us, without either inquisitiveness or rebellion. I felt that our knowledge would not make any difference, and that we had better leave questions of that kind to settle themselves in due course.*'

He began to study psychical phenomena and telepathy in the late 1880s, but would later have a more personal motive for his research. In 1884 he joined the London-based Society for Psychical Research. This society aimed to take a scientific approach to examining the claims of psychic and paranormal phenomena and aimed to better understand these areas through research and education. At the Society, he encountered Frederic W. H. Myers, who became his close friend. Together, between 1889 and 1890, they studied Leonora Piper, an American medium. They observed at sittings with local academics, including Gerald Rendall, the principal of University College, Liverpool, and Professor E. C. K. Gonner, an economics professor, that she was able to make extraordinarily accurate statements about their personal and family lives despite the care taken to hide the identity of the sitters.

In 1909, he published *Survival of Man*, a book in which he suggested an afterlife existed and evidence for it had been provided by mediumship. His next book, *Raymond, or Life and Death*, was published in 1916 and covered the seances Lodge and his wife had witnessed with the medium Gladys Osborne Leonard. Lodge's son Raymond, so the book reports, communicated with him and gave a description of his experiences in the spirit world. Raymond had a similar message to that of many other spirits, informing Lodge that people who had died were still the same people as when they had passed over. He also went on to say that there were houses, trees and flowers there and that the spirit world looked similar to Earth, except there was no disease.

Raymond, or Life and Death proved to be highly controversial. It was criticized for claiming that soldiers who had died during World War I smoked cigars and received whisky in the spirit world. However, who is to say that is not the case? In my view it would make sense. Some accounts from people who claim to have communicated with recently passed-over spirits do report that their new environment and experiences can be, for the initial transition period at least, quite similar to Earth life so that the spirit can acclimatize slowly to the new way of life. While this whisky-based criticism may say more about Victorian morality, or at least the appearance of it, perhaps the critics were disappointed and actually expecting the former soldiers to be playing on harps and singing with angels?

Just a few years before Lodge, as mentioned earlier, Sir William Crookes had become the first truly eminent Victorian scientist to attempt a serious scientific investigation into psychic ability to communicate with the afterlife. Let's consider some of the fascinating evidence he was able to produce from a series of experiments in the 1870s that gained plenty of attention but also approbation.

Oliver Lodge was president of the Society for Psychical Research from 1901 to 1903.

KATIE KING EMERGES

Professor Crookes was already familiar with the mental mediumship of several mediums when he came across Florence Cook, a physical medium who at just 15 could supposedly demonstrate complete materializations of spirits. Crookes set up a laboratory consisting of two rooms, one inside the other, with a curtain draped between them. The inner room acted like a medium's seance cabinet; Florence Cook would lay on a couch there and Crookes, with other invited witnesses, stayed in the outer room. Experiments varied in length; typically it would take 20 minutes to an hour for the materializations to manifest completely.

Crookes described his experiments to *The Spiritualist* newspaper on 5 June 1874: 'During the last six months the medium, Miss Florence Cook has been a frequent visitor at my house, remaining sometimes a week at a time. She brings nothing with her but a little hand-bag, not locked; during the day she is constantly in the presence of Mrs. Crookes, myself, or some other member of my family, and, not sleeping by herself. I prepare and arrange my library myself as the dark cabinet, and usually, after Miss Cook has been dining and conversing with us, and scarcely out of our sight for a minute, she walks direct into the cabinet, and I, at her request, lock its second door, and keep possession of the key all through the seance; the gas is then turned out, and Miss Cook is left in darkness.'

At the end of the manifestation time the curtain between the rooms was parted. A series of experiments in the 1870s would gain significant attention, when a mysterious spirit known as 'Katie King' emerged from the cabinet room in a white robe-style dress and head attire (possibly as a way of tastefully hiding areas of her body that did not need to be created in much detail). Katie King made repeated appearances to Crookes and others in his laboratory over a three-year period, and he later published his methods of research in the *Quarterly Journal of Science*.

Crookes reported that he managed to sample Katie King's pulse. He recorded that it beat steadily at 75, while Florence Cook's pulse was found to be at its usual rate of 90. He also listened to Katie King's chest, and could hear a heart beating inside. To all intents and purposes, Katie King appeared to be a solid human being, created within one hour!

FLORENCE WAS 'KATIE'?

The sceptic will, of course, say that Katie King the spirit and Florence Cook the medium were one and the same woman. In fact, Professor Crookes and other witnesses reported that at times Katie did appear very like Florence, and assiduously recorded his observations on this. In his book, *Researches in the Phenomena of Spiritualism*, he notes that Katie was six inches taller than Florence, her complexion was very fair while Florence's was darker, and Katie's skin was much smoother.

Closely inspecting Katie King's neck, he noticed that it was very fine to touch whereas a blister was prominent on the neck of the medium. He also noted that the spirit's ears were not pierced, whereas Florence habitually wore earrings. Crookes wrote, 'Miss Cook's hair is so dark a Brown as almost to appear Black; a lock of Katie's, which is now before me, and which she allowed me to cut from her luxuriant tresses, having first traced it up to the scalp and satisfied myself that it actually grew there, is a rich golden auburn.'

If, as some alleged, Florence was pretending to be Katie, she would have had to change clothes in the seance room. But Crookes and the many different witnesses who were present always saw both individuals together in the same room at the same time. Other sceptics have proposed that Florence had a secret accomplice, another medium who was staying with the Crookes family at the time. However, it would surely occur to Crookes and others that the second medium could be masquerading as Katie, especially as they had stood next to her and measured her pulse and weight. Besides, my guess, given the amazing circumstances of the materializations, is that this second medium would be in the room as one of the many witnesses to the phenomena. Based on my professional involvement with mediums and mediumship demonstrations, it's likely the second medium would have insisted on being present. When an excellent medium gives a demonstration, their psychic colleagues often want to watch them perform and learn from them.

Crookes reported that on occasions when he followed Katie back behind the curtain to where Florence lay in trance, suddenly the manifested spirit was no longer there. He took several photographs of himself arm in arm with Katie, and then posed with Florence in the same position to show the difference in height. Although there was an obvious power imbalance in this relationship between the eminent scientist and the 15-year-old medium, Florence received no payment and consented to undergo the various tests Crookes requested to prove her abilities.

Crookes studied Florence's abilities for three years and the daily experiments became so familiar that the ectoplasmic materializing spirit

Katie even became a friend to the Crookes family. After one seance, Mrs Crookes wrote, 'At a seance with Miss Cook in our own house when one of our sons was an infant of three weeks old, Katie King, a materialized spirit, expressed the liveliest interest in him and asked to be allowed to see the baby. The infant was accordingly brought into the seance room and placed in the arms of Katie, who, after holding him in the most natural way for a short time, smilingly gave him back again.'

A RISKY EXPERIMENT

Katie King is said to have agreed to a bold experiment, although this was not witnessed by Professor Crookes. At a separate seance with Florence Cook witnessed by a Miss Florence Marryat around 1890, a daring experiment was tried with Katie's permission, in which they sought to find out how long the manifested spirit could tolerate 'normal' light. Three gas lamps were lit and placed to illuminate Katie, who stood by a wall with her arms outstretched. Within seconds of being lit up, it was reported that the features on Katie's face began to blur, then her eyes sank back deep into her sockets and her nose melted away as if made from wax. Next, the frontal bone fell inwards and her limbs shrank and so did her form, until finally she sank into the floor with just her head remaining and finally she disappeared, similar to the Wicked Witch of the West's end in *The Wizard of Oz*. The experiment appeared to cause Katie no pain, and she 'lived' to return on other occasions. It's not clear how Florence the medium was affected. As mentioned earlier, bright light and natural daylight is seen as dangerous for a physical medium because it causes ectoplasm to be quickly reabsorbed into the body.

It is interesting to note that while spirits do not always manifest the whole body, Katie's heart and pulse was taken by Crookes, like a normal human being. How is it that a spirit can manifest internal organs but not the back of their head, hence the head coverings? And how does an animal spirit know how to form itself, as supposedly happened at the Scottish medium Helen Duncan's seances years later, when a spirit pony emerged? I suspect that in all cases, it is a combination of skills, not only the spirit's but also those of others directing the seances on the other side. As Katie's heart needed to be measured, perhaps the spirit world created it specifically for that one session. A newborn baby manifesting might be a creation of the spirit guides directing the seance rather than the baby's spirit, which wouldn't be able to consciously mould the ectoplasmic form on its own.

Various scientists have studied ectoplasm and described it as a kind of protoplasm, or colourless material comprising the living part of a cell, including the nucleus. If this is the case, the spirit world can extract this material from the medium and also the sitters, and even elements in the environment needed to form temporal (meaning physical) manifestations, like flowers or clothes on the sitters, rather like the

The materialized form of Katie King with William Crookes.

cloning of cells. As well as considering the spirit's material form, it's also interesting to ask who was Katie King in her physical life?

As mentioned earlier, some witnesses remarked that at times Katie resembled Florence Cook. However, one possible explanation is that materializing voices can initially sound like the medium, as they are using his or her physical makeup but over the course of the seance they develop further into their own characteristics. Physical materializations may behave in a similar way; as the spirit first attempts to manifest it uses the medium as a kind of template. So the template may resemble the medium in looks and voice as it starts communication, then gradually brings through more of its own characteristics as the session progresses.

ANNIE OWEN MORGAN AKA KATIE KING

When questioned by Professor Crookes about her former earth life, Katie said she was the daughter of 'John King', a spirit who presided over many other spiritualists' seances as a full manifestation. Her earthly name, however, was 'Annie Owen Morgan' and the surname of 'King' was a kind of title associated with a certain type of spirit with certain abilities or powers. Annie lived 200 years before Crookes in the reign of Charles II in Jamaica. Her father was a pirate – a famous one, as it would be revealed – who renounced his criminal activities and eventually became Lieutenant Governor of Jamaica.

A spirit also calling itself 'Katie King' manifested at a seance in Rome in 1974, with the Italian medium Fulvio Rendhell. This was photographed and although this spirit's clothes seemed very similar, her face was different compared to the photos taken by Professor Crookes. Of course, it could have been a faked session, but if it was true, this might explain the differences in each version of 'Katie'. Many mediums say that when channelling a spirit, the outcome is in fact a blend of the two consciousnesses, so characteristic traits of the medium and certain distortions can be present in the channelled material. The medium Jane Roberts' spirit guide Seth said that psychologically speaking, the meeting of Jane and the consciousness of Seth produced the final Seth personality. This 'paint-mixing' effect could account for the variations in the appearances in the Katie King spirit.

In fact, 'Katie King' and 'John King' appeared in other mediums' seances long before Florence Cook began communicating with her. John King first made an appearance at an 1852 seance held by medium Jonathan Koons at his home in Ohio in the US. Explaining this was his new name, 'John King' said he had actually been Henry Morgan, later Sir Henry, the Welsh privateer and plantation owner who died in Jamaica in 1688. After his death and subsequent arrival in the afterlife he realized how harmful his existence had been, and he was attempting to atone by returning to Earth to educate humanity on the continued existence of the soul. His daughter, Katie, had supposedly been an adulteress and murderer in her earthly life, so maybe this was also her intention. John King appeared in hundreds of seances with different mediums, and even instructed the famous American mediums, Ira and William Davenport, on how to build a seance cabinet!

THE BACKLASH AGAINST PROFESSOR CROOKES

After three years of research, in 1874 Professor Crookes reported his findings and results of his investigations into the mediumship of Florence Cook and her materializations of Katie King in the *Quarterly Journal of Science*. This caused a huge uproar and backlash in the scientific world, much of which had been looking forward to the eminent Professor Crookes disproving the 'trickery' of mediumship and the afterlife. Crookes was supported by some fellow scientists like the naturalist Alfred Russel Wallace, the physicists Lord Rayleigh and William Barrett and the engineer Cromwell Varley. The sceptical group was headed by William Benjamin Carpenter, the physiologist, who considered Crookes' research to be bordering on lunacy and also fraudulent. However,

Carpenter was actually interested in the potential of communication of mind, or telepathy. He also believed that the universe had a kind of divine cause, a sort of beginning created by a God. Yet this did not prevent him deriding Crookes' investigations into the supernatural.

Crookes invited the highly respected physicist Sir George Stokes, secretary of the Royal Society, to come and experience the manifestations of Katie King with his own eyes. However, Stokes, who was also a committed Christian, refused to do so, thus closing off a potential new channel of scientific advancement. Had men such as Stokes had the courage to truly open their minds to even the remotest possibility of an afterlife, they might have decided to see the evidence for themselves, and

William Benjamin Carpenter was sceptical of Crookes' research but had his own interests in telepathy and the supernatural.

maybe even have changed their minds. Or maybe they would have just turned on their heels and said 'No more.' Why is it that such naturally inquisitive individuals would not accept any invitations?

The UFO author and researcher Richard Dolan offers some insight on this question. In an interview he stated that he gets many letters and emails from respected scientists who are now retired. When they were employed they would not even acknowledge the subject of UFOs when it was discussed in their presence, but after retiring they felt more comfortable expressing their genuine and great interest in the subject. Quite simply, they didn't want to jeopardize their professional status by appearing to entertain things outside the scientific 'norm'. I suspect that something very similar was happening to Sir William Crookes and other such open-minded scientists who were going against the norms of their era.

Many were no doubt privately interested, especially in the latter part of the 19th century, when spiritualism became something of a 'craze' – and even Queen Victoria was said to have consulted a medium following the death of her beloved husband Prince Albert. But in an time of fast-developing scientific discovery, grappling with the newly discovered invisible forces such as radiation and electromagnetism, maybe it was too great a leap to consider the possibility that these were not the only invisible spectrums and other, paranormal, beings existed alongside them. A highly moralized and often performatively religious Victorian society would also probably find it extremely difficult to comprehend, never mind publicly express, such a fundamentally challenging idea as the so-called dead not lying in the ground and waiting for judgement, but being free and able to return and speak with them and touch them whenever they chose.

THE EDDY FAMILY

While it does not involve a scientifically trained individual, a similar story was happening in the US in the later 19th century, again as the public became increasingly interested in spiritualism and concepts that differed significantly from key tenets of the Christian faith in which most of them grew up and were expected to live by. This strange tale occurred in the small farming town of Chittenden, Vermont. Reaching a peak of activity in 1874, the farmstead home of the Eddy family – brothers William and Horatio and their sister Mary – was seemingly a hotspot for encountering physically materialized spirit beings.

The case gathered press attention when one of the investigators into the assassination of President Abraham Lincoln, a man named Colonel Henry Steel Olcott, became involved. Olcott was an ex-army officer and journalist who was initially a sceptic of spiritualists and their claims. He was perhaps a fitting choice to become the leading researcher into the Eddy family along with their apparent visitors from other worlds.

During the American Civil War, Olcott was a special investigator who rooted out corruption and fraud within the military. It was this experience that enabled him to approach the Eddy seances with an investigative eye. He would even bring in engineers and builders to investigate the house where the materializations occurred, to see if there were hidden doors and floors that could be used to trick those witnessing the materializations. The Eddys themselves were by all accounts farming people with very little formal schooling. They were suspicious of strangers, perhaps understandably due to their mistreatment as children by a harsh father who initially tried to stamp out what appeared to be their natural mediumship skills. Later he would actually sell his children to travelling shows to entertain crowds, where they were further mistreated by a showman who 'owned' them. When their father died, the siblings returned from the travelling shows back to their home. During the day they worked the farm. However, during the evenings, they demonstrated their remarkable skills to paying guests, who were said to have witnessed spirits playing instruments, along with materializing babies and adults, Native Americans, late friends and family of the bereaved, Africans and people who spoke other languages were also said to have manifested in front of Colonel Olcott and the audience.

Of course, a sceptic would argue that Mary, Horatio and William Eddy had experienced the 'business' of spiritualism at first hand in

Colonel Henry Olcott, one of the investigators into the assassination of President Abraham Lincoln, also turned his eye to examining the paranormal goings-on of the Eddy family.

travelling shows, and understood the level of public interest meant there was money to be made, even among the poor. However, after visiting the Eddy family for four months and sending written weekly reports back to the newspaper he worked for, Olcott concluded that they were either the cleverest fakes ever or genuine mediums. Such was the effect of this experience on him, that he later went on to form the Theosophical Society in New York in 1875. One of the aims of the society was to investigate unexplained laws of nature and the powers latent in man. Ideally, Olcott would have perhaps benefited from the help of a scientist. In today's world, thanks to the likes of Olcott, more scientists and researchers are coming forward and talking publicly about their science-based testing of paranormal phenomena, and starting to establish some fascinating theories about reality and the universe that could help to answer some of the most fundamental questions about the supernatural.

CHAPTER EIGHT

DOOR HANDLES TO A NEW FRONTIER

For around 150 years the field of quantum physics has evolved as scientists have studied the fundamental composition and the behaviour of nature's building blocks, matter and energy, to help us understand how our universe works. This need arose from the gap between the prevailing scientific wisdom of the time and how scientists observed matter and energy actually behaving. This is why, for instance, they would adjust their viewpoint of light from a kind of electromagnetic wave to an object with the characteristics of both waves and particles, or 'wave-particle duality'. They are still grappling with a 'theory of everything' that can describe the whole universe, from vast planets to inconceivably tiny 'quantum' particles.

Just as we know new theories of the universe will inevitably emerge, and entirely new planets or even solar systems will be discovered, some scientists, writers and other thinkers are challenging opinions on the nature of our reality, and that of others. This chapter delves into some new ways of thinking about whether the afterlife exists and where it might be – billions of light years away, much closer to home, or even within the sub-atomic particles that surround us. Some extremely smart people are putting forward science-based ideas about the existence of other dimensions, that could also make us re-evaluate the basic physics of our 'normal' world and, therefore, what 'paranormal' means. Seth, the entity who came through the medium Jane Roberts, said that mankind has its hand on the door handle of a new frontier, and at some point we will turn that handle and open it. Unexplainable things have long been coming through that door to us, but maybe sometime soon we will open it and even step through, accepting both the evidence that we are not alone and the challenge to know what is on the 'other side'.

SPIRIT INTENT

One modern-day scientist claims his research demonstrates that the spirit world proves its existence by its intent and will; that is, he has set up experiments using a medium and the spirit world has frequently gone well beyond the original intent of that experiment. Gary E. Schwartz, author of *The Afterlife Experiments*, *The Truth about Medium* and *The Sacred Promise*, is Professor of Psychology, Medicine, Neurology, Psychiatry and Surgery at the University of Arizona and Director of its Laboratory for Advances in Consciousness and Health. His conclusion arises from his work in recording the existence of spirits, spirit guides and even angels.

As an aside, I personally experienced a version of Gary's theory when the spirit of my mother Margaret came through during Ouija board sessions. The two mediums there had a clear protocol in place, that the spirit moving the glass should announce themselves, initially by the first letter of their Christian name. Before they could ask all their introductory questions, under the movement of Margaret's consciousness the glass whizzed around and spelled out 'Hi Son!', much to everyone's surprise. When Margaret was asked about meeting up with her own parents, rather than just saying 'yes' she expanded beyond the question, replying, 'My mum came and met me.' This shows that there was an excited, independent personality moving the glass, with answers that surprised the sitters, and that Margaret's spirit had clear intentions beyond the established protocol. In a second board session she then broke off midway through answering questions and went out of her way to thank the mediums for their work. She also reassured Mike, one of the mediums, that 'they' would look after his sister, who at the time of the reading had terminal cancer.

Like my mum's spirit, Gary Schwartz observed that the spirits he worked with also asserted themselves, sometimes taking charge of the experiments he was trying to conduct. One of them, a scientist Gary actually knew in her lifetime, was also a researcher into life after death. So it made perfect sense to Gary that this spirit showed up not long after her passing and decided to help out in his continuing research.

SUZY OBSERVES FROM SPIRIT

Gary's former research partner, Suzy Smith, passed away aged 89. According to Gary she was looking forward to proving to him and the rest of the world that she lived on in the spirit world. Within a month of her passing she had reached out to him via a medium who lived on the opposite side of America in the Pacific Northwest. My guess is that Suzy chose a medium far away from Gary in order to rule out accusations that a local medium could have known him personally. This medium, referred to as 'Joan' by Gary, had been psychic since childhood and her extraordinary abilities appeared to attract spirits to her in droves.

After Gary's former colleague Suzy showed up at Joan's house and asked her to contact him, Gary received an email he wasn't sure about. Part of him was suspicious, thinking it could be a prank or a hoax by a sceptic. Even so he opened it, curious to see the messages that Joan was receiving from Suzy on the other side. These were a mix of what he called 'watching-over-me' information, where Suzy seemed to be observing Gary and reporting what he had been doing, and prediction readings, where she would warn him of things that might need attention. He felt this was pretty accurate information, but he wanted to conduct more research. He and Joan agreed that every day she would email him messages she had received from Suzy the previous evening, after Suzy had observed Gary at home and told Joan what he had been doing.

In an effort to put Joan through her paces, Gary did not follow his usual evening routine. One evening he decided to watch baseball on television while reclining on his bed and eating a Chinese takeaway meal, none of which he typically did. Joan's email came through the next day, announcing that Suzy had told her Gary was eating a foreign food. Suzy also mentioned baseball and that Gary was not eating the food at a table or in a restaurant but in a reclined position. She also warned that Gary might have a problem with a tyre on his car. Sure enough, the next day, Gary came out of his laboratory to find out that his car had a flat tyre, which hadn't happened to him for several years. Gary acknowledged that Joan could have arranged with someone to deflate the tyre, or used some kind of psychic remote viewing ability. (It's worth noting that Joan was not receiving any payment for working with Gary.) However, another genuinely incredible instance of the spirit world asserting itself was to happen later.

A MESSAGE UNDER ANAESTHETIC

One woman, Jackie, wrote to Gary about an incident that occurred to her while she was having an operation in hospital. (Gary changed the woman's real name and those of the other witnesses.) The facts could be verified by those who witnessed it, all medically trained professionals. Jackie required a lengthy and complex operation that would take several hours. After coming round, she asked the nurse on duty how the procedure went; the nurse replied that it had gone well, but hinted that something odd had happened during the operation that upset some of the medical staff who were present. Concerned, Jackie made a point of asking the surgeon who performed the operation to tell her precisely what had occurred.

Reluctantly, the surgeon explained that as it was a long operation, part of the way through Jackie was in need of further anaesthetic in order for the procedure to continue. The anaesthetist, Robert, was about to administer it when Jackie suddenly sat upright on the operating table, pointed to him and cried out 'Robert!' She then said she was 'Julie' and that he was not to blame himself for what happened, because she was already dead when he found her and he could not have saved her. Robert was shaken and distressed and had to leave the operating theatre. He later said that he believed his late wife Julie had come through and called out to him, using Jackie's body as her medium of communication. He explained that a year earlier he had come home from work one day to find that Julie, a fellow doctor, had cut her own throat and although he tried his best, it was too late to save her. Ever since he had suffered from terrible feelings of guilt over her death.

In theatre everyone would have worn a mask, full gown and cap, so Robert would have been unrecognizable to everyone apart from his colleagues, yet Jackie, or whatever was controlling her, picked him out. It appeared that in spirit Julie, who wanted to get through to her husband, spotted an opportunity to take over the body of someone who was already in a trance-like state, which a 'normal' medium would take some time to reach.

She may have timed her appearance just as the anaesthetic was slowly wearing off, but while Jackie was still sleeping. Any longer and the body she needed might have been too deeply sedated to make Jackie sit up, which as a doctor Julie would probably have understood. Gary Schwartz offered this incredible case as an example of intent on the part of the spirit making the evidence for the existence of the spirit world all the stronger. Those in spirit take over the situation, in a way that lets those on earth know that they are still around and asserting themselves when the need arises.

Of course, this experience did not happen in laboratory conditions. But if true, it was witnessed by highly trained medical professionals, although the surgeon was not keen to relate the experience to Jackie and the medics did not put their names on record, due to the privacy of all concerned. Even if doctors and other scientists do not discuss such paranormal experiences publicly, these phenomena are not going to go away.

DIAL 'PMP' FOR SPIRIT?

Gary Schwartz's afterlife investigations continue, as director of the Soul Phone Project. As mentioned earlier, this university-based team of academics and engineers is working on the seemingly impossible – devices for communicating with 'postmaterial persons' (PMPs), starting with one where the user can question a spirit communicator who will be able to text back a simple yes or no answer.

If this can be perfected, future plans for the technology include a keyboard that humans and spirits can operate just as they would when messaging on any smartphone. Long term the goal is that this can be then developed into the Soul Voice, an audio device that would allow users to actually listen to and talk 'live' with those on the other side, or maybe even others who have never even lived on Earth! It's hoped that Soul Video communication will be the final stage of development, where you will be able to see those on the other side, in much the same way as you might see friends over Skype or Zoom.

If the Soul Phone Project's technology was being refined in a secretive government laboratory funded by vast 'black' money budgets the public are not privy to, it would no doubt have progressed further by this point in time. Is technology such as this a threat? Imagine the possibility of being able to talk directly to President John F. Kennedy, or even Lee Harvey Oswald, or the political havoc and scandal that certain famous people could cause by coming through with their version of events! It seems unlikely that powerful elites would allow this to happen. My fear for such a technology, as exciting as it is, is that a higher level of power or vested interests would step in and prevent its development, one way or another.

INGO SWANN, REMOTE VIEWER

It is perfectly reasonable to assume that governments have considered, if not actively explored, the potential offered by otherworldly entities, mediums and those with psychic abilities such as second sight or remote viewing. It appears that experiments with remote viewing, an extra-sensory perception of images and other sensations in a different location to the psychic individual, have been funded. One example of an undisclosed project involved an American remote viewer named Ingo Swann (1933–2013). In his own book *Penetration* (2011), Swann said that he worked for the US intelligence services in secret in the 1970s, using his psychic abilities to mentally spy on (then) Soviet installations or bases.

Swann said he was later recruited to try and remote-view the Moon by a mysterious 'Mr Axylrod', who instructed him to mentally visit certain co-ordinates on the lunar surface and report what he could see there. Swann reported back that he could see humanoids who appeared to be naked and engaged in mining the Moon! Who or what these humanoids were is not known, but it is a possibility they were some kind of alien being using our planet's Moon for their own resources. If the US governmental agencies have been using psychics, then it's highly likely their counterparts in China, Russia and other nations, as well as ally nations like the UK, will also have investigated these methods or developed their own secret projects. They may be refining some kind of psychical 'drone' projects at this very moment in time!

THE 'BORROWERS'

Rather than helping themselves to the metal and other mineral wealth of our physical world, alien and other paranormal beings could be borrowing from us in other more subtle ways. This is the intriguing theory put forward by John Keel, journalist and author of the famous *The Mothman Prophecies*, his real-life account of paranormal events in a small town in 1960s West Virginia.

He posited there is some kind of reality beyond ours, and the inhabitants or consciousness of that place occasionally intervene in our reality. Keel was sure that UFOs and aliens from space were actually more of a type of character created to interact with our reality. They were a kind of intermediary or interface creation to penetrate our world, like a puppeteer creates a wooden puppet to perform a play or story. He suggested that UFOs emerge into our world and borrow 'ingredients' of our reality at an atomic level in order to manifest themselves here, albeit on a temporary basis. This idea is reminiscent of some accounts earlier in the book of spiritual beings 'borrowing' ectoplasm from mediums and sitters at seances so they could appear as physical beings to walk around and talk with sitters. Could this be the process that UFOs, faerie beings, angels and all other paranormal beings use to come and go from our reality? Maybe they emerge from their universe through what Keel called 'windows', or portals, dazzle us with their displays and knowledge, then lose their tenuous physical grip on this world and 'zap' out again.

According to Seth, the spirit guide of American psychic Jane Roberts, when UFOs emerge into our world they are trying to adhere to the rules of their reality while also trying to conform to the rules of ours. This would account for witness reports of UFOs appearing to morph and change shape; they could be struggling with maintaining the form they take in their world and the one they are depicting here. You can think of a foreign visitor arriving in another country, with a different language and social etiquettes. They would try and learn the language, observe local laws and try to blend in. However, their own accent and background would still show through to a degree. It is likely to be the same with Keel's UFOs, except they come from another reality, so when their physics attempts to blend with our physics, it distorts, like a foreigner may distort the language they are attempting to speak. So it does not flow smoothly but breaks, or is misunderstood. The visiting UFO may not appear as a solid craft of one shape, but change or morph into something else, as if it's trying to adapt on the spot.

John Keel saw UFOs not as alien beings but as intermediaries from the spirit world, created to interact with our world.

So as spirits, ghosts, UFOs and elementals emerge, they borrow or steal some elements of the material world, but to an extent they also merge with it. It's like they have become a dual being or object, part earth and part astral. Keel believed anything of a paranormal nature was from these realms and should not be trusted, even spirits in a seance. I myself believe that although Keel was on the right tracks, he never mentioned ever attending a demonstration of mediumship or a seance. This was, I believe, a weakness in his theory. To my knowledge he never had a message relayed to him via a medium or attending any kind of physical seance. Had he done so, he might have yielded to the idea that not all spirits coming through in a psychic demonstration or seance are the bad guys! Just as in our world there are all kinds of people, the same good, bad and indifferent people will reside in the spirit world once they have passed over.

HOW MANY DIMENSIONS?

From my own research I have come to believe there are many worlds beyond this one we call Earth, not just in space but also as other dimensions, planes, or 'levels of reality' as the spirit guide Seth described them. In theoretical mathematics, the development of 'string theory' (in simple terms a single way of describing the fundamental forces of nature, gravity and electromagnetism) led to the concept of there being 11 dimensions, although I suspect that is just the beginning. Seth explained that reality is like one thread of cotton suspended at two points of a rectangular box-like frame. Coming off this strand are other strands of cotton that all go off in different directions to the original, and from these further strands, eventually going through the frame and beyond it into many other theoretical frames. In other words, many different realities impinge on ours, some closer to our world than others.

Some of these realities are very far removed, and can be called higher planes of reality – this is where Seth said he was from. The spirit world, or the afterlife as some refer to it, is a level of reality just beyond ours. A comparison can be made with white light: when seen through a prism it is in fact made of up different colours, or frequencies. Some are visible to the human eye but eventually waves become invisible infrared, ultraviolet, X-rays, gamma rays and others.

GOOD VIBRATIONS

The different levels or planes of the spirit world can also be seen as a series of different frequencies or vibrations. Some of these can be 'viewed', usually by those who are sensitive enough to perceive these 'broadcasts', which are thoughts and impressions translated down through these phenomena into the mind of the medium, or perceived as entities in a room. A witness may be able to pass their hand straight through what appears to be a solid person in the room, whereas that entity can actually pass through a solid door or floor. Just as radio broadcasts pass through walls to your radio receiver to eventually be converted to audio, where a radio presenter can be heard speaking, so these supernatural channels pass through our dimension to be momentarily perceived by those with the right receiving equipment.

Some thinkers suggest that time exists all at once: that every time period is actually the present. Therefore it may be that if the conditions are right for us to see a ghost or spirit, from their point of view *we* may also be a ghost. Some witnesses of hauntings have noted the ghost itself seemed surprised. We mentioned before that paranormal researcher and author Irene Allen Block wrote that while she and her husband were visiting her son in his new house in London in 2004, she came face to face with a maid in Victorian uniform coming through the door. Irene gulped in shock as she almost bumped into her – and the maid looked back at Irene, equally aghast! Within seconds, the maid had vanished. Irene heard no sound, but clearly remembered the maid's shocked expression. Her son, Jamie, used to see her often standing at the top of this big staircase when he used to come home from a night out. She would just stand there watching him as he came through the door.

In Bath, England, around 2010 historical researcher Andrew Mercer was looking for a particularly antiquated book in an old library building. He noticed a movement in his peripheral vision and, wondering who else was in the often unvisited area of the library, turned to see a man walking down the aisle in old-fashioned dress including a top hat. The well-dressed man looked directly at Andrew with a surprised stare and turned a corner. Andrew followed him down the aisle and around the corner, but the gentleman was no longer there.

Spirits that are not sighted under controlled seance conditions tend to be less material, and more astral-like, that is more a projection of consciousness broadcasting into our world from afar. They might be able to communicate but usually are not solid and the projections tend to last only for a few minutes at most. As already described, spirits can become solid through the mediumship of physical seances, under specific controlled conditions and if the energy levels are right. In this case a spirit can use ectoplasm to form a temporal but very solid physical body.

CONNECTING THE DOTS

Addressing the question of what paranormal beings are naturally raises further questions: how are they able to communicate and intersect with us? Where do they actually live or reside? And how, apparently, can we sometimes be seen by these other spirits in their own time frame? A theory does exist that helps to connect the dots and it originates from a one-time sceptic of the afterlife. The late Michael Roll from Bristol, England founded the Campaign for

Philosophical Freedom, which explores non-religious arguments for survival after death. He changed his sceptical views after his deceased father's spirit returned to him in materialized form, with help from a physical medium named Rita Gould, in 1983, and began to campaign publicly on his belief in life after death. Rita Gould had agreed to be tested and filmed by a professor at Edinburgh University, using modern equipment including infrared video cameras to capture the materialized physical forms of spirits, but later withdrew, claiming her life had been threatened if she participated in these experiments. Looking elsewhere for substantial evidence, Roll met Ron Pearson, a Derbyshire-based engineer, applied physicist and former university lecturer in thermodynamics and fluid mechanics. Pearson helped Roll by formulating his afterlife theories, which Roll subsequently published on his website and in later books, and also appearing on radio and TV together.

CHALLENGING THE BIG BANG

In the 1980s Pearson developed a thesis that challenged the 'Big Bang' theory, the widely accepted view that our universe came into being nearly 14 billion years ago when an infinitesimal point of heat suddenly expanded in an enormous explosion of energy and that it is continuing to expand, as described by Einstein's general theory of relativity. Ron Pearson believed the theory was flawed, for instance due to evidence of some stars being much older.

Over several years he developed an alternative theory based on collisions between two forms of energy, negative and positive, a process creating 'filaments' of energy that enabled the universe to keep expanding at an increasing rate. These gave rise to a grid structure, similar to the brain's network of neural pathways, through which energy travels in 'quantum waves', with spikes of energy creating the matter of the universe. This vast, self-powering switching system is fully connected to every part of itself as a universal mind.

SUPER-MIND AND SUPER ENERGY

A 'super-mind of space', said Ron Pearson, could create different matter systems, or realities, all co-existing in the same space but all tuned to different quantum-wave frequencies. As 'sub-minds' or fragments of the 'super-mind', we can only tune into one matter system at a time. When the body dies, the mind as a separate entity simply tunes into one of the remaining matter systems and continues to survive beyond the physical universe. Pearson reasoned that the human brain may actually be a mere interface mechanism that enables the mind to pilot the body. Therefore, he concluded, there is no justification for arguing that consciousness vanishes on brain death.

Another enquiring scientific mind also pointed to the existence of a super intelligence. David Ash, author of numerous books on quantum physics, mysticism and consciousness, believes this super intelligence comes from forces of 'super energy'. He argued that the sub-atomic particles that make up all elements of our physical world are not material grit but whirlpools of light. Each of these spinning whirlpools are in fact universes beyond our present one, but spinning at a higher vibration, beyond the speed of light. They are all right here, right now, simultaneous existences within our own. Ash has said, 'I am predicting that in these worlds of super energy beyond the speed of light there are going to be living intelligent beings and because our world is part of their world they can see us even if we can't see them... the laws of physics are exactly the same on each plane, the only difference is the speed of energy.' Therefore, sightings in our reality of faeries, angels, ghosts and spirits are all part of his 'super physics' philosophy. Everything is made of light and distinguished by different speeds of light. We are in the slower lane, and occasionally we get overtaken by something in the faster lane and catch a momentary glimpse of it.

'DARK MATTER' ZONES

As part of his thinking on the space 'super-mind', Ron Pearson also refers to 'dark matter' (the scientific name for the invisible areas of space that neither emit nor reflect light), and Michael Roll to 'ether' (a Victorian term) to explain the unknown parts of the universe. This concept may help to explain the strange appearances of other phenomena, beyond the spirit world. The ether or dark matter universe may be inhabited by faeries and other paranormal beings such as centaurs. Occasionally it seems these other realities can intersect with ours, enough to be perceived. They may not all show up on our normal cameras but their inhabitants may impinge into our world as etheric forms, just enough for those with sensitive minds to perceive them. Similar to David Ash, he says these worlds are right here, right now, not 'out there'. We walk among them, and in turn they walk among us. Just occasionally, we are bestowed with just the right environmental and mental apparatus to encounter them.

David Ash argues that spinning whirlpools of light make up the fundamental matter of our physical world.

What precisely is dark matter? As mentioned, modern science still has no idea what comprises around 80 per cent of our universe. Although this dark matter cannot be directly seen, it is thought to have effects on visible objects. Some scientists interpret such things as black holes (dead collapsed stars) as dark matter because they no longer emit light, whereas other researchers believe it is responsible for other, paranormal occurrences. For example, are UFOs actually ghosts in the dark matter machine?

'NON-HUMAN ORIGIN'

In 2023 former US Air Force officer David Grusch spoke to Australian journalist Ross Coulthard prior to his testimony to the US Congress's national security sub-committee investigation into 'unidentified anomalous phenomena' (UAP), or UFOs and recovered crashed or retrieved craft. In a groundbreaking interview, Grusch went on record to say that he was blowing the whistle on the whole UFO cover-up and wanted Congress to investigate the issues he was raising. He spoke about how the US and other countries have retrieved crashed craft and technology that are not of this world. Grusch was part of the UAP Task Force, a public-facing government group set up, supposedly, to investigate claims of UFOs, similar to Project Blue Book. (This was a US Air Force investigation set up in the 1960s to explain away the UFO phenomena. It was closed down, having stated there was no mystery to uncover and even attributing some sightings to swamp gas or balloons! As sightings continued, the pressure has ramped up on successive governments to fully investigate UFOs. In an attempt to appease the public, the US government set up the UAPTF (Unidentified Aerial Phenomena Task Force) to hold public presentations every six months to explain their findings.

Grusch worked for the UAPTF, but believed information was being held back from the task force, thus presenting a distorted idea of what was really happening. Since then, he has spoken out about his belief that information on aliens or beings of 'non-human origin' has been held back by government authorities, stating that, 'elements of the Intelligence Community improperly withheld or concealed alleged classified information' from Congress. Grusch emphasized that he has not been used in any way by any agency or individuals and that he spent four years considering the information he was being allowed to know. He was given very precise information from various groups that strongly corresponded to each other, strengthening the case that what he was being informed of, was at least part of the truth. He would later make further statements to members of Congress away from the prying eyes of cameras and the press – the full details of which we can only speculate about.

Some commentators have pointed out that distances in space are so vast that it would be impossible for any UFOs, even if they existed, to get from 'there' to here. However, this is based on an assumption that these craft or beings, whatever they are, are from other planets or galaxies. Grusch speculated that given the vast distances in space and even from Earth to its closest neighbours, aliens or ETs are in fact beings from other dimensions. He also spoke about how quantum physics might explain how it was possible for other dimensions to interact with us. He seems to be one of the first government officials to discuss 'beings from other dimensions' rather than from another galaxy as such in a public setting.

Prior to Grusch, UFOs were thought to be objects from other star systems. J. Allen Hynek, an astronomer at Northwestern University in Evanston, Illinois, who had been involved with projects Sign, Grudge and Blue Book, in the 1960s, concluded that a small fraction of the most reliable UFO reports gave definite indications of the presence of extraterrestrial visitors. Hynek, previously a sceptic of such things, eventually founded the Center for UFO Studies in 1973 (CUFOS), which continues to investigate the phenomenon.

It is fascinating to think that alien craft are indeed in the possession of the United States' and other countries' governments, and indeed, it has been suggested that such craft have been assembled or created at an atomic level.

David Grusch testifies before the Senate on the Unidentified Aerial Phenomena Task Force in July 2023.

APPORTS

It appears that creators of extra-terrestrial craft or UFOs may be able to manipulate matter. This is suggested by certain reports involving recovered UFOs where the recovery team has entered a craft measuring about 40 ft (12 m) wide, but inside the interior stretches out to the size of a football stadium, just like the Tardis of Dr Who. Dr Steven Greer of the Center for the Study of Extraterrestrial Intelligence and the Disclosure Project has covered many of these types of cases and reports in his films and interviews with UFO witnesses.

Also like the Tardis, whoever is piloting these craft are thought to somehow manoeuvre them through dimensions or portals from one universe of matter to another. This sounds rather similar to the concept of 'apports' during spiritualist séances, where objects are taken from one dimension and pushed through to another. Reports of these phenomena typically involve objects created here, like coins or newspapers from the past or even flowers. These materialize into a seance room, usually falling from above the recipients and, apparently, become permanent in our world. Supposedly they dematerialize from one location in our physical universe, move into a space wormhole or portal, then emerge from there into the seance room, perhaps within minutes of them vanishing from another part of the physical world. In the Scole experiments of the 1990s, a group of researchers and psychic mediums claimed to have conducted a seance where they were in contact with the deceased medium, Helen Duncan, who managed to apport or bring through an original newspaper from her time that covered the story of her trial. The newspaper was checked for authenticity and found to be from the 1940s. These events usually also bring forth an argument that some kind of trickery or sleight of hand is involved. Nonetheless, most mediums are usually very happy to cooperate with those that want to check and test them for any fakery. They are keen to understand the phenomena themselves. Apports usually drop from the air and appear quite spontaneously.

One totally unexpected apport is believed to have suddenly appeared in Mark Johnson's house in early December 2022. His wife, in her early fifties, tragically passed away from a blood clot in late November of that year. Mark, originally from California but now living on the East Coast of the US, is a paranormal podcast host and researcher. Mark relates: 'We had just come back from my wife's funeral. Her cousins were going to stay with me, so I went to get the guest room bed ready for them. That's when I saw the coin, a US .25 cent piece (a quarter). It was a state quarter, part of a series that was supposed to honour each of the 50 states. When I found it, it was tails up, showing the state of Colorado. She [his late wife] hated that state since that's where I stayed with my family when we were separated for a time. So to me that was her way of getting my attention and to know it was her.' Mark believed the coin was sent as an apport from his recently deceased wife as a sign that she was still around.

Coins seem to be a common thing to apport through. Perhaps it is because they are small, but also contain clues, like messages from the possible sender. The year of the coin is always present, and the country of origin. Mark's wife had only just passed, so an old coin would have been out of place. But a fairly recently minted coin (2006) with a clear pictorial message of Colorado, is almost as good as sending her signature. Why didn't she just send her signature? It seems from research, much easier for the spirit world to grab something from our world and send it through a portal of some kind and have it fall right under our noses.

As with physical mediumship, where ectoplasm is 'borrowed' from the medium for the spirit to materialize, it could be possible that extra-terrestrial visitors use substances taken from our world, to make a temporal spirit form as they enter our world, rather than travelling physically from another galaxy. This is not to say that extra-terrestrials are spirits of the dead, but they could be what *The Mothman Prophecies* author John Keel termed 'ultraterrestrials' – from some other place that he could not place in our time and space. Many abduction reports include aspects where the abductee claims to have been removed from their home through solid walls, without having to open a door, supporting the idea of extra-terrestrials or aliens, whatever their place or time of origin, are able to manipulate matter and time.

In one account of a UFO abduction case from the USA in 1974 uncovered by UFO writer Preston Dennet, the abductees asked the occupants of the UFOs where they came from. They answered back quite cryptically that they came from a place that the humans knew nothing about. In fact, many accounts of humans interacting with these beings seem to indicate that the 'aliens' are rather cagey about their origins. Some say they are from other star systems, and others do not seem to want to divulge their origins at all. Maybe 'other star systems' is the simplified explanation of something far more complex than they think humans would be able to comprehend. Some may come from other universes we have not yet identified, or from other dimensions effectively seconds away in time.

Whatever that answer may be, just as they seem to be aware of us, we are also hopefully now on the cusp of being able to watch them back. And exactly as would be the case if people were to generally accept the existence of the spirit world, this would cause a major shift in our consciousness – our own 'super-mind', if you will. Are we about to mark a new era in humankind?

CONCLUSION
THE GHOSTS OF TOMORROW

> 'There is a whole moral revolution taking place at this moment and affecting minds; after having been developed for more than eighteen centuries, it is nearing its completion, and will mark a new era in humanity. The consequences of this revolution are easy to predict; it must bring, in social relations, inevitable modifications, which it is in no one's power to oppose, because they are in the designs of God, and because they arise from the law of progress, which is a law of God.'
>
> Allan Kardec, founder of Spiritism

These words were written in the 19th century to describe spiritism, also called spiritualism by many. Today it is a global movement but its aim is unchanged, to bring light and understanding into the world. In spiritism we can do this because our spirit, or soul, or essence, continues, before and after our physical body lives in this world. When we die our spirit becomes discarnate and returns to a spiritual plane where it can, hopefully, continue evolving and learning. We aren't good or evil – we simply *are*.

So if mankind is a spiritual being, evolving with all the other animals of this Earth, is it possible that alongside him other beings outside our band of visible light, have always been co-inhabitants of our world?

A SPECTRUM OF BEING

Humans can perceive only 2.5 per cent of the electromagnetic spectrum, or full wavelength of light. The rest, including infrared, ultraviolet and gamma rays, is outside our range of vision. Does this mean all those elusive beings – faeries, ghosts, spirits, UFOs and more – are lurking in another part of the spectrum? Are they evolving alongside humans through the millennia yet have only been glimpsed occasionally, in certain conditions or by the sensitive few, whose reports have filtered down through the centuries to become the legends that have seeped into our consciousness and formed part of our cultural DNA? And is this all we have, these scant experiences of the past that have formed into stories? Or do we have more pertinent up-to-date evidence of this paranormal world? For me, the answer is fortunately yes we do!

There is photographic evidence of paranormal entities, both creatures and objects that may be inhabiting the invisible spectrum of light. It is only in the last 70 years or so that we have had the technology to tap into perhaps just one aspect of this unseen world. Since 2008 Nik Hayes, a researcher in Oxford, England, has been photographing strange things over his house with a specially adapted digital camera that captures images in the ultraviolet and infrared range. He took inspiration from the research of author Trevor James Constable, who from the 1950s to the 1970s took many photographs using infrared filters, and found strange organic shapes manifesting in his film camera exposures. Some appeared to be UFO-type structures, and others more creature-like in appearance.

QUESTING FOR 'INVISIBLES'

Trevor's work inspired modern researchers like Nik to continue investigating this strange new world, although most of the scientific world has turned a blind eye to this research. Nik believed he had been

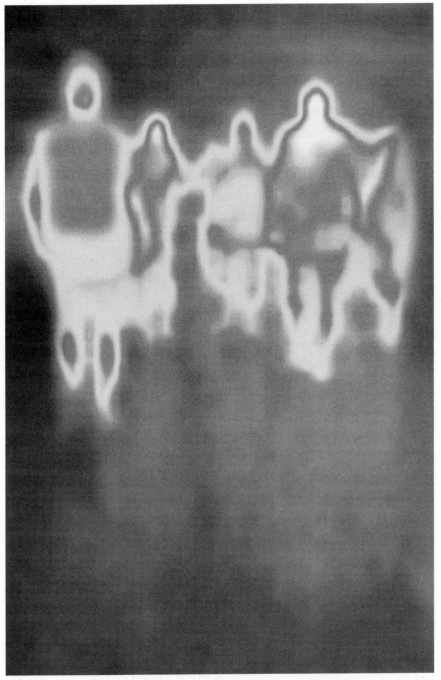

Human beings are unable to perceive large parts of the electromagnetic spectrum. Could faeries and spirits be lurking in the infrared or ultraviolet bands?

watched by the authorities since he began his experiments. When he sent his camera to the US to be converted to infrared it was held for nearly six months while US authorities checked out his background and camera.

Fortunately it was returned intact, and Nik continues his daily experiments, studying video footage frame by frame and screen-capturing strange anomalies. Some of the things he has photographed are quite bizarre: one being looks like a flying valve tube, others like strange jellyfish in the sky. What exactly are they? Maybe nothing more than artefacts in the digital video composition? Perhaps, but Trevor Constable was convinced other life forms exist in the upper atmosphere that are as yet undetected by humans. So maybe our technology is on the cusp of officially discovering them, and more. Nik found that building a 'cloudbuster' somehow attracted the strange objects down close enough to his house to be photographed. (This multi-tube device was devised by the Austrian psychoanalyst Wilhelm Reich to make rain, using a kind of universal life force he called 'orgone energy'.) Today Nik continues to search the skies for further anomalies and has presented some of his findings in his first book, *Quest for the Invisibles*.

CONSCIOUSNESS BEYOND BIOLOGY

Another organization believes its research is 'touching the invisibles' and, in addition, making things beyond our normal perception visible by photographing them – not strange creatures of the upper atmosphere however, but the unseen universe of the afterlife.

The French Institute of Spirit Research and Experimentation aims to demonstrate that consciousness exists beyond biology, or the body. Taking guidance from 'automatic writing', where a spirit will control a person's hand and write clear messages itself, the group has brought together various technologies to produce evidence of spirit intelligence, including images, videos and spoken words.

The group asks a medium to sit in a small chamber filled with misty air, then shines laser beams through the mist in that chamber, and records the process. Its short bursts of video images show faces, words and letters appearing over the mist, which cannot be written off as chance or face pareidolia. Face pareidolia is how some people might concoct faces in clouds or on tree bark or other natural objects. The spirits communicate through automatic writing in order to describe the experiments taking place. For example, the group has reported a spirit explaining, 'The mist inside will be resonated by induction. The cameras will then record interference waves made visible by the laser light, itself in vibration. The experimenter will be part of the experiment and will be able to observe the variations of the mist and therefore our interventions.' Similar objective images have been sighted of spirits in smoke rising up from ashtrays, so it may be possible to use mist or smoke as a medium upon which to somehow impress spirit images, like one might draw in wet sand.

ANOTHER PHYSICS

The spirits coming through continue to explain about how the technology of communication will change in the future and also at the same time, harness the power of AI. In one case they noted, 'Artificial intelligence is the first step towards the intelligent transformation of eternal omnipresence. The trans-communicators of tomorrow will also use sensors, not for the production of human sounds, but to allow spiritual omnipresence to take shape. Not in biology, but in complex systems of structures, what you call digital. Additionally, the synchronization we are talking about is another physics that rules your space.'

So it seems that AI plays a part in the new phase of communication with other worlds, as well as other technology such as infrared cameras. The same spirits from the French team talk using a synchronization of another physics that rules our space. This suggests an entirely different form of physics that we are only just perhaps starting to discover. Maybe they could be talking about 'string theory' or the ether that Ron Pearson postulated about life after death worlds.

In the famous Scole Experiment, the spirit communicators there had to apparently harness the power of a reality beyond their own level of occupation to produce certain physical phenomena. So it's like taking an electric transformer, which takes alternating-current to other circuits and stepping down, or reducing, the amount of the current so that its power moves things in our world or communicates in some way, either visually or orally or both but utilizing a power of a higher force. Otherwise, it would be too powerful, but it's transferred through to the other reality. So this may mean that these future AI communications devices might work in our reality, but using physics and realities way beyond our understanding; AI might even design itself to make the communications work. Spirit or non-biological entities may also be able to interact with the AI, take it over and then harness that intelligence, fine-tuning its specifications to become super-intelligent communications devices. Like Gary Schwartz's assertive spirits in his experiments, they will be able to judge what is required and take charge of the technology. This power would presumably be very intelligent and operate beyond our known universe, at a much faster frequency than us.

The late science fiction author, Arthur C. Clarke stated in 1962: '*When a distinguished but elderly scientist states that something is possible, he is almost certainly right. When he states that something is impossible, he is almost certainly wrong.*' Ironically then, it was Clarke's well-received British TV programme of the 1980s, *Arthur C. Clarke's Mysterious World* which hinted that he himself had reserved notions about the paranormal. He indicated in the series that somehow, mediums were not either bringing back the dead, or if they did, the dead could not articulate their previous earthly skills through the medium very well. It was one thing as a writer he was not prepared to accept – that your skills in the afterlife somehow diminished. While he introduced such a programme with interesting stories and accounts, it seems he did not really believe much of what was shown.

British physicist Lord Kelvin, one of the most innovative scientists of his generation, who achieved presidency of the Royal Society towards the end of the 19th century, made such confident assertions as '*X-rays will prove to be a hoax*', '*radio has no future*' and '*heavier than air flying machines are impossible*'. We can see how even mainstream established science is far from infallible. While we should not believe all claims of the paranormal, we should also realize that the sceptical claims of scientists against it should be taken with a pinch of salt.

A new generation of scientists with more open minds are required to carry on the work of Lodge, Crookes and others, to illuminate the hidden shadows of our world, and maybe find other worlds within worlds. I believe that eventually the evidence will become more widely accepted as changes in attitudes occur. New scientists will group together and put their names to the new research and move us forward, with the help of those on the other side. It may take time, but there are indications that this is already happening. We may not be able to capture a faerie being in a jar, but we are on the edge of dialling into the variations of probable universes, or planes of reality that are just outside our perception at present.

Max Planck, the German theoretical physicist whose discovery of energy quanta, the fundamental discovery of quantum physics, won him the Nobel Prize in Physics in 1918, said, 'A new scientific truth does not triumph by convincing its opponents and making them see the light, but rather because its opponents die, and a new generation grows up that is familiar with it.' Science has traditionally tried to measure and analyze things. Seth, Jane Roberts' guide, said that what science fails to realize is that its measurements will never be correct, because its measuring sticks are part of the universe it is trying to measure. Everything within our universe is part of the system. Even the most accomplished theoretical physicists, including Planck himself and fellow Nobel Prize winner Richard Feynman, claimed that it wasn't possible to truly understand quantum physics. It's foggy around the edges, so to speak. Just as we begin to see through that fog, we meet another barrier and so once again must adjust our sensors and theories to pull what is behind it into focus. We will come to realise that as much as we are in the universe, the universe is also in us. Already, the next generation of scientists have stepped boldly forward.

INCONTROVERTIBLE EVIDENCE

In February 2022 the New York Academy of Sciences published a paper, 'Guidelines and standards for the study of death and recalled experiences of death – a multidisciplinary consensus statement and proposed future directions', signed by 18 English and American scientific researchers, which in effect stated there is incontrovertible evidence that when we die, that cognitive part of us goes somewhere else. In other words, when we die, we do go on to another kind of existence. Perhaps we ascend into the ether of Michael Roll or the dark matter worlds of Ron Pearson, or maybe we spin in the super energy worlds of existence identified by David Ash. Whatever it is and wherever it is, no matter what it is called, mainstream science will eventually have to link up its ropes with this alternative physics and work together to ascend the mountain of new thought. They will open up the door at the top to peer through and see that the ghosts of the past have become the ghosts of tomorrow. A birth of a new paradigm has begun.

INDEX

A

Academia de Estudos Psychicos (Academy of Psychical Studies) 153

After We Die, What Then? (Meek) 177

Afterlife Experiments, The Truth about Mediums and the Sacred Promise, The (Schwartz) 220

aliens see UFOs

Allen, Irene 229–30

Allen, Jamie 229–30

ambulance hauntings 53–6

apports 236–9

Armstrong, Louis 107–8

artificial intelligence 245–6

Ash, David 232

astral travelling 61, 95–7

Attwood, Ken 175

B

Bacci, Marcello 179–81

Baird, John Logie 202

Bander, Peter 175

Barham, HMS 120, 121–2

Barnum, P.T. 134–5

Barros, Jose de Camargo 155

Bartlett, Ross 130

battlefields 77

Bennet, William 167

Bennett, Alan and Diane 182

Benson, Hugh 188

Block, Irene Allen 79–80, 229–30

Bonomo, Leo 164–5, 171, 176

Borgia, Anthony 188

Bradley, Herbert 168

Brandine, Joan 95–7

Buckmaster, Nigel 167

Butts, Robert 75

C

Calling Earth (documentary) 180

Carpenter, William Benjamin 213–14

Carrington, Hereward 124

Catchpole, Mrs 144

centaurs 27–30

Chaplin, Paul 39–40, 41–4

Chapman, George 64–7

Christian attitudes 187–91

Churches' Fellowship for Psychic and Spiritual Studies (CFPSS) 189

Churchill, Winston 9, 109–11, 122, 171–2

Clarke, Arthur C. 246

computer hauntings 87–91

Constable, Trevor James 242
Cook, Florence 207–15
Coventry, C. B. 200
Crawford, William Jackson 124
Crisp, Quentin 109
Crombie, R. Ogilvie 20–1
Crookes, Philip 194
Crookes, Sir William 194–7, 202, 207–15
Crossley, Alan Ernest 166

D
d'Albe, Edmund Edward Fournier 124
Davenport, Ira and William 213
de Meneses, Bezerra 155–7
de Souza, Ganymede 154
Delaney, Christian 77–8
Dennet, Preston 238
Dixon, Jean 26
Dodleston messages 87–92
Doris, Winifred 130–2
Douglas, Matthew 119
Doyle, Sir Arthur Conan 9
dreams 39–44
dryads 35–6
Duesler, Mr 198–9
Duncan, Helen 102, 104, 105, 116–26, 237

E
ectoplasm 123–5, 143–4, 145, 163–4, 167, 171, 210–11
Eddy Family 215–18
Edison, Thomas 160–1

Edward, John 126, 138
electronic voice phenomena (EVP) 172–9, 181
Ellison, Arthur 182
Ernetti, Pellegrino 173

F
Feynman, Richard 247–8
feys 34–5
Firebrace, Roy C. 121
Flint, Austin 200
Flint, Leslie 149, 163–7, 171–2, 176, 189–90
Fontana, David 182–3
Forer, Bertram R. 134
Fox, Mark 26–7
Foy, Robin 182–3
Fox sisters 194–203
Foy, Sandra 183

G
Gale, Jack 33–4, 45
Garrod, Eileen 145–6
Geddes, Alex 130–1, 132
Gemelli, Agostino 173–4
ghost boxes 183–4
Gilchrist, Gina 37–9
Gilchrist, Lyndon 37–9
gnomes 25–7
Goddesses, Guardians and Groves (Gale) 45
Goligher, Kathleen 124
Gonner, E. C. K. 205–6
Gould, Rita 231
Greene, Betty 163

Greer, Steven 236
Grusch, David 234–6
Guardians of the Dead (Kinsella) 184
Gurney, Edmund 13

H
Hale, Peter 175
Harris, Richard 112
Harrison, George 108–9
Hayes, Chris 131, 132
Hayes, Nik 242–4
Heaven and Hell (Swedenborg) 203
Herald of Free Enterprise 67–9
Higginson, Gordon 142–6
Hood, HMS 120–1, 122, 123
hospital hauntings 52–6, 57–67
Hyde, William H. 202
Hydesville rappings 194–203
Hynek, J. Allen 235

I
Institute of Spirit Research and Experimentation 244

J
Jobs, Steve 186
Johnson, Marjorie 26
Johnson, Mark 237
Jones, Alex 151
Journey of Psychic Discovery, A (Crossley) 166
Journeys Out of the Body (Monroe) 61, 151

Julian, April 22–4
Julian, Mary Rose 22–4
Jung, Carl 39, 41
Jürgenson, Friedrich 173–4

K
Kardec, Allan 241
Keel, John 226, 228, 238
Keen, Montague 182
Kelvin, Lord 247
Kent, Roger 80–1
King, John 212–13
King, Katie 106, 207–16
Kinsella, Philip 32, 132–3, 183–5
Kirkwall, Carrie 59
Koo, Wellington 168
Koons, Jonathan 213

L
Lang, William 64–7
Lang, William Cosmo Gordon 188–91
Lee, Charles A. 200
Lennon, John 108–9
Leonard, Osborne 162
Life in the Unseen World (Borgia) 188
Lincoln, Abraham 216
Lodge, Sir Oliver 205–7
Lovelock, Ralph 175

M
Macey, Mark 175–6
Marconi, Guglielmo 202
Marryat, Florence 210

Marshall, Dr 165
Martindale, Harry 81–4, 86, 87, 92
Maxwell, Ronald 175
May, Gray 36–7
Mayer, Robert 175
McNeill, Kathleen 123
mediums 102–27, 129–57
Meek, George and Jeanette 176–7
Mercer, Andrew 230
Milligan, Scott 105–6
Millins, Claire 40–1
Mirabelli, Carmine 153–7
mirror hauntings 56–7
Monks, Dave 46–8
Monroe, Robert 61, 96, 151
Morrison, Herbert 122
Mothman Prophecies, The (Keel) 226, 238
Mueller, George Jeffries 177–8
Myers, Frederic W.H. 13, 205

N
Nanji, Dinshaw 165–6
NASA 7, 42
Native American spirits 30–2, 33
nature spirits 33–5
Nibiru 44
Nordic aliens 150

O
Odale, Steve 21–2
Olcott, Henry Steel 216–18
Olson, Joan 85–6
O'Neil, William 176–9

out-of-body experiences 61
Out of this World (TV programme) 91
owl spirits 37–9
Oz factor 10

P
Pan 20–1
Parsa, Hussain 19
Patel, Stephanie 186–7
Pearson, Ron 231–4
Penetration (Swann) 225
Phantasms of the Living (Gurney, Myers and Podmore) 13
Piper, Leonora 205
Plack, Max 247
planets 42, 44
Podmore, Frank 13
portals 32–3, 44–6, 67–8, 91–2
Pressi, Paolo 179–80
Price, Harry 122, 124
psychic doctors 62–4
Psychic News 105, 143, 144, 189

Q
Quest for the Invisibles (Hayes) 244

R
radiation belts 151–3
radio transmissions 179–81
Randi, James 139
Randles, Jenny 10, 11
Raudive, Konstantin 174–5, 176
Ray, Kate 34–5

Raymond, or Life and Death (Lodge) 206
Rendall, Gerald 205
Rendhell, Fulvio 212
Researches in the Phenomena of Spiritualism (Crookes) 208
Roberts, Jane 36, 74–6, 80, 101, 111, 152–3, 220, 247
Robertson, Tricia 146–7
Roll, Michael 230–1, 232–3
Roman soldiers 81–7
Rosna, Charles B. 196
Rowe, Gary 91
Rust, Dr 125

S
Sakellarios, Stephen 138–9
Sanders, Debra and Alex 92–5
Santi, Franco 180
Schwartz, Gary E. 186, 187, 220–5, 246
Scientific American 160
Scole Experiment 151, 181–3, 237, 246
Scottish Spiritualist Society 117
seances 102–16, 119–27, 143–4, 148–9, 150, 153–7
Secrets of Heaven (Swedenborg) 203
Seeing Faeries (Johnson) 26
Seth 74–6, 79, 80, 152, 220, 226, 228, 247–8
Seth Material, The (Roberts) 36, 74–5
Seth Speaks (Roberts) 75, 80

Shanes, Ian 67–9
Shaw, Conan 190
Simons, Owen 44–5
Sitchin, Zecharia 42–4
Smith, Brian 97–9
Smith, Gordon 136–7, 138
Smith, Suzy 221–2
Smythe, Colin 175
Society for Psychical Research 90–1, 125, 162–3, 182, 205
Solomon, Jane and Grant 183
Spiricom 176–9
spirit guides 102–27
spirit voices 159–91
Stanley, David 175
Stewart, Albert 119, 121, 123, 125–6
Stockwell, Tony 126–7
Stokes, Sir George 214
Stone, Abbie 57–8
stone tape theory 76–7
Story of Psychic Science, The (Carrington) 124
Survival of Man (Lodge) 206
Swann, Ingo 225
Swedenborg, Emanuel 203–5

T
Things You Can Do When You're Dead!: True Accounts of After Death Communication (Robertson) 146
This Morning (TV programme) 136
Thomas, Charles Drayton 161–3, 166

Thompson, David 171
Trajina, Carlos 180
tree spirits 35–7
Turner, Daniel 140–1

U
UFOs 10, 46–9, 149–51, 226–8, 234–9

V
Valiantine, George 168–71
Valle, Jacques 10 (SPR) 10
van Overloop, Haak 167
Vertical Plane, The (Webster) 91
Viana, Octavio 154
Voice of Spirit, The (Bonomo) 171
Voice Transmissions with the Deceased (Jürgenson) 174

W
Ward, Margaret 12–13, 220–1
Warden, Tina 59
Webster, Ken 87–92
Wells, H.G. 41–3
What Happens When We Die? A Lawyer Presents the Evidence for the Afterlife (Zammit and Zammit) 148
White, Dave 53–7
Whymant, Neville 168–71
Wiseman, Richard 91
Withers, Frank 75–6
Wollaton gnomes 25–7
Woods, Sydney George 163
Wright, Jackie 141

Z
Zammit, Victor and Wendy 148–9, 151–3

PICTURE CREDITS

Alamy: 11, 18, 68, 118, 174, 211, 236

Library of Congress: 43

Shutterstock: 14, 23, 24, 27, 36, 54, 65, 82, 93, 162, 227, 233, 243

Topfoto: 164

Wikimedia Commons: 20, 29, 90, 103, 110, 135, 145, 152, 156, 161, 170, 185, 191, 195, 199, 204, 207, 214, 217